LOVE PASSAGES

A Poetic Love Series

*Titles available in the Love Passages series
(in reading order):*

Hot Pink Nail Polish and a Broken Heart

Inkwells of Love

LOVE PASSAGES

A Poetic Love Series

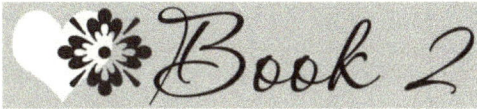

Book 2

INKWELLS OF *Love*

Ms. Tabu

First Edition by Mic2Soul Publishing, February 2020

Book cover design: LLPix Designs

Author Photograph: Robert Cooper

ISBN-13: 978-0-9861728-2-3 (Paperback Edition)

ASIN: B084T9H791 (Kindle Edition)

Printed in the United States of America

2 0 1 5 9 0 6 0 6 6

This book is printed on acid-free paper.

I dedicate this to all the love warriors out there still fighting to keep real love alive.

CONTENTS

"I read once that ancient Egyptians had fifty words for sand and the Eskimos had a hundred words for snow. I wish I had a thousand words for love, but all that comes to mind is the way you move against me while you sleep and there are no words for that."

- *No Words* by Brian Andreas

"The minute I heard my first love story, I started looking for you, not knowing how blind that was. Lovers don't finally meet somewhere. They are in each other all along."

- rumi

Baby Where You At?

Baby where you at?
Could you be somewhere
caught between the seasons
on the cusp of change?
I know your heart is beating
I just don't know your name
Still, I believe in our love without delay
Nothing comes before its time
But I'm wondering about you and I
So curious to see where we will meet?
Your first impression of me
Will we automatically know
this is meant to be?
Will we encounter things like jealousy and envy?
Will you empower me when life devours me?
Of course you will, but I'm seeking confirmation
longing to feel the feeling of amazing
Soul mating, beyond physical embracing
I don't have any expectations, except for this to be
the best thing that has ever happened to me
I know it will be
Tell me, are you thinking about me
somewhere beneath the moon,
sun setting on the beach?
Could you be in your room
hiding out from the winter too?
What season is it currently for you?
Do we even live on the same coast,
in the same state, or country?
I've accepted the concept of no limitations
when it comes to the one for me
Where there is a will there is a way

That's how I know our love will find its way
Am I getting any hotter, am I even close?
Baby, I don't want to live this life alone
These nights been so cold on my own
Out here on the grind,
on the hustle trying to get mine
Trying to survive is like a puzzle
Evidently pieces will always be missing
because as we grow, the picture will be different
Well, new beginnings are cool
as long as they are leading
to me finding you, you finding me
When a man wants a woman he will seek
so baby come to me
Come to me
Show me what it is like to be
truly, unconditionally
loved for the inner me
Lovers but never enemies
Best friends before we get married
You'll be the reason
giving birth doesn't scare me
I'll be the reason
being a father secures you
Always there for me,
I'll be there for you
How beautiful it is
to give not to receive
this forever receiving gift
Neither you nor I stuck with
the short end of the stick
The balance of love exists

so long as we maintain it
Baby, I'm surrounded by so many faces
But none of them look quite like you
Not that I would know either way if
I'm here without a clue, waiting for a sign
Usually just chilling, but tonight it's on my mind
Why is every other guy coming at me with a line?
But the man God's got for me is somewhere
caught between the seasons,
on the cusp of change
I know your heart is beating,
I just don't know your name
Still, I believe in our love without delay
Nothing comes before its time,
but I'm wondering about you and I
So curious to see who you are spiritually
Although I wonder about your physicality,
I'm more interested in your design mentally
Will we need an ice breaker or will it just flow?
Imagining our first conversations and our first jokes
Our first love making, inspiring my first poems
for the first chapter of our life together
What is your day of birth?
Forget astrology.
I just want to know which day
to thank Mommy for delivering you
to one day find me
I'm missing you when I've never
had you beside me
but you've always been inside me
like the constant trace of a memory
Remember me

I've always loved you from afar
Thought I was following my heart
Traveled among the stars but then got lost
Figured I'd just stop
to make things easier for both of us
I know you'll show up
whenever the universe chose for us
but it seems like you are
somewhere caught between the seasons
on the cusp of change
I know your heart is beating
I just don't know your name
Still, I believe in our love without delay
Nothing comes before its time
but I'm wondering about you and I
Baby where you at???

That Kind of Love

She liked the kind of love
that made ripples in her heart
A passion so deep, its energy
told stories to the clouds
of new shapes their shadows
invented in candlelit rooms
through a language of vibrations
ancient communications
nature only knew
The kind of love that kissed with its mouth open
in the pouring rain, silhouettes lit by the glow
of a moon that discovered its own soul
only in the reflections of their connection
as its shine began to grow, bright
like the power of one million poems
A love that altered everything it touched
Magnifying beauty, every time it blushed
as the universe responds
to every design of his and her "us"
Infinite combinations, all equating
to the palette of their creation
Experiencing a many new "paintings"
from the same paint in
a different technique,
texture or shading
Tapping a new vein of inspiration
from the unchanging source
The kind of love that breathes
lives, gives... more
It can be tasted, seen,
felt, even smelled...
through spiritual senses

More than just the
"When he speaks,
she finishes his sentence",
phenomenon
More like when her heart beats,
his answers
with complete synchronicity
as she lies upon his chest
listening to the sweetest song
she's ever heard
in a rhythm quite familiar
yet from the outside looking in,
it all can sound so new
It was the kind of song
about that kind of love
and that was when
she knew.

The Angel Watcher

There he sat...
observing every detail of her
Not in the creepy way, of a peeping Tom
or in the psychotic way of a stalker
but in the way of an angel watcher

He noticed the things about her
no one else ever did
The way her eyes changed colors
or that defined line in her bottom lip

The way she shared a secret
without ever really telling it
but in a way he could hear it
if he closely listened
and he always did... listen

He listened to the tone in her voice
that reminded him of forgiveness
even though sometimes
the fleshly preference
would have been conviction

He listened to the heartache
that gently tucked itself
behind her bottom lashes
and he could almost hear
her tear fall back into its lid

He listened to the stories
of her body language
written like riddles

in her movements
and motions, so complex
yet so simple

He heard her wings
open and close
Sometimes he thought
he heard them breaking
in the middle of a poem

But he watched her,
the way she pieced them
back together
as her essence sparkled of
hidden treasures
never found
or so she thought

She thought
nobody knew the truth
about who she was
that she could pour out her soul
with one hundred percent proof
Still, they would only see
the little piece they cut
Put it in a box
to call it what they want
when all he saw, was love

Sometimes he wanted to touch...
as he felt the reflexes of his tongue
wanting to speak

He dreamt to tell her
the way her presence
had changed his identity

But see,
he was scared
to lose himself in
the absence of
the right time

He thought,
he might damage
a moment that was
meant to be divine

After all, approaching
an angel wasn't something
he'd been taught in all his life

Most of all,
he didn't want to taint
the same purity
that made him complete
when he was once empty

But her ability
to rise to the skies
and find some tranquility
no matter how many times
she'd been hurt blew his mind
in a way that renewed his sight

In a way that brought
the dullest hues to life
She was the angel that
mused him to fly

He watched her on the Mic
as she performed the way
he'd seen her write
So free, almost carelessly
but yet so carefully

She'd made a napkin of his heart
A spare piece of paper, of his soul
Rushing through him the words of an angel…

and she didn't even know.

His Button-Down

I liked the way he wore his, button-down
Wondered how he unbuttoned down
What was his style
Did he start from the middle and work his way up?
Or was he sometimes versatile
You know the way a man does the simplest things
can say a lot about how he may treat his lady...
Funny as this all sounds...
and something about those buttons
made me want to be his baby doll
Maybe it was how his arms felt
when they hugged me close
or my imagination thinking about the dimples
that hides beneath his clothes on his back, real low
where sweat would form small puddles
during sessions of making love
I liked the way his chest pressed it
without being so tight that it was deliberate
Envision this...
handsome brown skin with some turn me out lips
Made me wonder how he kissed...
How he...
How I wished!
But... I don't even know him
and here I am picturing in slow motion, unbuttoning...
delivering my fingertips to his outfit
And although it sounds like
I just wanted to see the brother naked...
the truth is, I wanted to see the brother period!
I wanted to see him, at romantic dinners, candles lit
I wanted to see him, at a museum or an exhibit

I wanted to see him, at a family gathering like Christmas
I wanted to see him, at worship services, praising Him
I wanted to see him, in my dreams and awakening
I wanted to feel him in my sleep, vacationing
to a place so deep, that we can't see surfaces
I want him to swim with me,
until our pain doesn't hurt within
I wanted to be the reason he
no longer has a look of sadness
and I wanted to unbutton his eyes too
Unbutton his mind, and take off his shoes
Unbutton his pride, his lies, and his truth
Unbutton everything he holds inside
and see what it all looks like
Too many buttons baby,
you need a woman to help you
I hoped he could hear these thoughts
running through my cerebrum
I've watched him change like love's seasons
Seen him in the daytime and in the evening,
always wearing a sexy, classy, make me want to
bring him home to Daddy button-down
and he just doesn't know how he teases my soul
I already know my favorites of his wardrobe
It's pathetic, I know!
Especially since I'm far from desperate...
could have my pick but if you didn't know
I've already chose

I wonder if he wonders about my clothes
when I'm rocking Mics at shows

If he likes the way I match
and have a mind of my own
Expressing myself shamelessly
in patterns and prints
I wonder if he ever
wore a certain button-down
hoping I would notice and I did,
or do I even exist?
When I keep disappearing between his lids
awaiting a perfect moment of eyes contacted
so they can have a conversation of their own
Oh no... I'm losing control,
wanting him to lose a button inside my home
from the passion in between
each word that was spoke
without saying a thing

I want to hear his heart beating
faster and faster with each button
and the order doesn't matter
Just get it off so he can feel me close,
heart to heart, lost like buttons in the sand
where no one knows
Leaving hints and lover imprints
to something unforgettable
But I know before we "button down",
we've got to button vows
And oh how I long to know now
how he plans to unbutton my buttons,
we all have a few
Wondering if he feels the way I do
about letting them buttons loose

I'd better stop before I fall in love with you
Now you're coming over to talk...
got to keep my cool
as much as I want to unbutton you
It's much too soon to be discussing
such a subject with you
wouldn't want to be judged
for being honest with you
but then I catch you
looking at the buttons between my breasts
and I let you become
just as infatuated with my buttons
as I am with yours
but I hope that you want something more
when I need a man who also serves the Lord
and when I saw the cross chain around your neck
I gently pulled it my way and even caressed
that very top button as I felt your breath on my neck
Your muscles flexed and all of this began
because of those buttons
Not to say he's the only man
who knows how, to rock a button-down
but that he's the only man
I want to rock with inside and out
and I'm interested in how he likes it done
right down to the very last button.

I Would

I would...
Put on a fancy dress, open back,
elegant, hugging my curves just like that
I'd even put my hair up, now that's a change
Get the stilettos on, manicure, and pedicure
make a brother go insane
when I walk down that staircase
just to see the look on his face

Amazed...
like he just saw
the most beautiful woman
in this whole place
Just to make him take
my hand and say,
"You look stunning,
let me lead you the way!"
Kiss it gently and
bring me to the ballroom
to celebrate

Wait...
I would catch him staring at me
throughout the night
Be the woman of his dreams
make them come true tonight
but deep down inside...
I'd be hoping he could see
past my physical beauty
They say beauty doesn't last
but for a moment in time

When you look into my eyes,
what are you bedazzled by?
Does it even matter
that I have a mind?
Is it more than a master-plan
to unlock my thighs?

Still I'd...
spray the perfume on my neck
put on my most feminine under garments
For you darling, I'd lace the modern day corset
to emphasize each breath from my breasts
I'd wear a necklace with a locket
just to make you wonder what's in it

I'd gloss my lips to perfection
Mascara my long lashes
Eyeshadow to match my dress
Make sure I don't forget the lotion
from head to toe
but deep inside I'd be praying
you'll want more than sex

I would...
wear all my secrets on my gloves
if it were the key into your deepest love
I'd wear those diamond earrings,
never worn yet
Anything to grab your attention,
even for moments
I'd be all the lady you ever asked for...

I'd cross my legs when I'm seated
I'd wait for a man to ask before
I went to the dancefloor

I'd savor my dinner without a rush
I'd wait to take a picture
until I'm freshened up
Excuse myself,
push my seat in
grab my pocketbook
and softly strut

I'd pray by the sink
that you were waiting for me
that you'd be the gentleman of my dreams
that you'd save the last dance for me
Out of all these beautiful ladies...
you'd take the chance with me

I'd make sure
I looked just right in the mirror
Before re-entering to gather in cheers
I would hold my glass like a lady should
I would handle myself with utmost class,
make it look so good
but deep down inside I'd hope
that I wasn't being misunderstood

See, I'm here for more than just a crush
My heart came here
hoping to be found by love

But if everything I've done
wouldn't be enough,
then I would do it all until it was

Until sparkling wine
became your sparkling eyes
looking deep inside mine
as you'd ask my profession
and I'd pause, mesmerized
See, I'd create the first impression
but I wouldn't sell you lies
I'd tell you I'm a poetess
and hope your hands
wouldn't lose their grip
I'd hope these weren't the words
to spoil a moment like this
I'd hope you could look past
a room full of doctors, lawyers
and respect my business

But I'd go on to say...
"I went to college
for Business Management,
soon to pursue my Master's in..."
and pray you'd interrupt me with a kiss
and that you wouldn't laugh at the fact
that my life purpose depends on the tips of pens
pencils, Microsoft, publishing programs,
writing, performing, recording poems
I'd pass you my business card and say,
"I also do show productions, which I host,

you should come to one of them!"
I would then in some orderly fashion
attempt at asking you the same question
but it wouldn't make a difference to me
if you were a doctor or musician

Don't you see my love?
I'd love you all the same
I would do all these things
just for you to know my name
but deep down inside I'd pray
that you'd be there now
and through the fame
that you wouldn't run away
at the thought of having a lady
in the spotlight, every day
that you'd leave me with
the time to explain…

None of this would mean a thing anyway
if you didn't come with the ring
and let our love just fade away
because you are the missing piece to my dreams
Without you, I couldn't be complete
So while I would do anything
for you to notice me…
tell me darling, what would you do for me?

Fresh Air

Baby do you feel the way I feel?
Tell me am I crazy or is it really real?
Do I sound cliché when I say
the first day I met you I thought that I felt
you were the one, some kind of higher connection
Makes me want to tell someone to get to stepping,
good or bad, *good or bad*
Some people are just gatekeepers to lead us
to those who are meant to serve
bigger purposes on our path
I have recognized the clear distinction
between what I need and what I had
as I'm gravitating toward all the reasons
why we linked just when we have
All the sure signs the universe has shown
Now I just want to nurture these seeds to grow
Resisting the need to force what isn't in our control
It will come when it will come, let's just be vulnerable
while calling out for protection
from the physical repression others try to bring
to tamper with progression, damaging our wings
A little pinch of faith goes a long way and then some
Everybody thinks they play the game,
when it really plays them
Trying to have our way
instead of remaining patient
Now all I can say for certain
is that I am taking every single cue to…
Rock with you
Ride with you
Walk with you
Vibe with you

I told you before I want to fly with you
soon as I came out of my cocoon, baggage free
somehow I knew you'd be waiting for me
naturally, it was mutual
the balance is complete
No more or less when it's really real
plus you inspire me to do things like finish that
"Sunshine and Poetry" piece
that's been stagnant with no right words to fill
but it's like sunshine and poetry
how you are making me feel
every time I...
Rock with you
Ride with you
Walk with you
Vibe with you
Not to mention, you always make me laugh
whatever it is we are laughing at
doesn't matter to me long as we're smiling
If it's my number you're dialing...
I'm picking up, asking how your day was
not just for the small talk, I genuinely care
That's the sincerity between us
whether the simplest of subjects
or the most intellectually productive
I'm equally stimulated
because I want to...
Rock with you
Ride with you
Walk with you, vibe with you.

Just a Kiss

Modern perception has me longing for an old-school love
Back when, it meant something more than just...
just a hug, then a kiss... and now it's "just sex"?
"Just" a breath of life you shared,
a moment that was never even promised to be there
So on that notion, while you've got me open...
let me properly inform you,
that this will never be just one of those things
that when your lips press against me
it will never lack meaning in the depths
of those places other men have left empty
and if just sex could have kept me
by now I'd be tied down, but see...
I've never been the "just sex" kind of lady
so these think they invented it brothers
don't persuade me
'cause the only thing they are really inventing
is a situation of babies born out of poverty
with ladies they consider crazy
Well, of course she's "crazy"
because what was "just" to you, was more to her
and women were never put here
to mother grown men to mature
but still I realize the odds are against us, these days
For a man not playing games, I do give thanks
Although there are no exceptions,
there should never be a woman who expects less
Regardless of the minimum standards that have been set
due to social conditioning, leaving substance repressed
But do know that for you, my lips will never be deaf
They will always hear the messages sent
through the vents in your chest,

passing through my breasts, entering my heart
as my beats learn your language
so that we're speaking on the same wavelength,
moving in one rhythm
It will never be just a coincidence
that I'm in your bedroom kissing you inch-less,
parts of your body you didn't even know existed
And I will never come by just to visit
without my ultimate purpose being
to spend these moments that may be our last
with the only man on the planet
who makes me laugh, quite like that
Makes me moan, quite like this
Makes me want to tell everyone I know,
that I'm in love with him
See, this was never just a crush, just to "bust a nut"
See, you've got me busting notes,
I never knew could be sung
See you've got me writing poems 'cause…
you inspire me!
This was never just another poetess pimping poetry
because frankly baby, getting men isn't my difficulty
but getting men isn't what moves me
when getting is nothing more than getting
It doesn't mean for keeps
Yes, I love the way you kiss me but
the beauty of this is much more than skin deep
I feel your lips in colorful prisms of my soul
where my aura changes like a mood-ring
as rings of afterglow keep me afloat
Never felt this feeling before
but see, feelings can come and go

But this became more than just "feel"
This became real, destiny already written
This wasn't just something different
just because it wasn't the same
This is different because it is a love pumped
from the creator's veins
Impossible to underestimate
Not even an option to contemplate
Even when our flesh tried
to come up with reasons why
Quickly our spirits force us to exercise obedience
Praise the most high
This ain't just an illusion of the mind
As you and I
U N' I TE,
I realize, this ain't even just making love
This is giving love, living love
It's much bigger than us, so please…
never think that it was ever "just", to me
Save that lifestyle for everybody
and let's just BE the YOND,
far from just snake-charm
Lustful venom may do the job
but never for too long
You are more than just my heart,
you are my entire being
Never just a cause,
you are the reason.

Mind Readin' U

Mind readin' U, you readin' mine
Let's stop playing games for a while
All of this small talk
is just an appetizer to the real entrée
Not to say, it isn't
quite the boost to our appetite,
like an aphrodisiac
to get the mood right, right?
But in between each line,
I'm mind readin' U,
don't mind U Readin' me
Just think it would be nice to
get a bite of that too
Please don't think I'm rude,
interrupting this light hearted lingo with you
Just kind of think it'd be cool to…
build on the foundation on which we mingle
where the possibility for pyramids exists
If we put our minds to it,
something divine will begin
If we can just shift that way
for a few minutes
Let those thoughts manifest
into our beautiful existence
Suppose this is it, our last days
Suppose we just keep skippin' past
all the things we want to say
What if I never kiss your lips
and this moment drifts away?
Mind Readin' U, so I'm confident
this street goes two ways
Mind Readin' Me,

you probably know what I'm about to...
Yes, I was about to...
Yes, that's exactly what I'm thinking!
But how'd you...
know it all?
Respondin' to my thoughts,
just like I am to yours
Mind Readin' U, communicatin' to my heart
Longing to hear it too so, can we talk?
Enough about the weather
and all these silly things
Inside of me there is a sun always shinin'
no matter what the season brings
This is what you've done to me,
do to me, doing... as we speak
Brings me peace, falling deeply
in sweet harmony
just by Mind Readin' U
so imagine what we could do
with this telepathic canvas we seem to share
if we just allowed each other to
the higher understanding of this spiritual affair
Allowing it to exist in the physical realm
Bringing these words through our lips,
giving them power to be felt
on whole new levels
You know we can't just settle
for this simple chitchat
when we were given these
vessels that long to give back
Did you get that?
Should I resend that?

Or is that the reason why,
you're lighting all the candles,
illuminatin' all our vibes?
It's time to free our minds
express all the things
we've held inside
Sometimes readin' minds
just ain't the same as
hearing it on the outside
where we can bring things to life,
connectin' words with passion in the eyes
Look into mine...
readin' minds won't be needed tonight
Time to tell the real,
breakin' open the seal
Speaking reality into
all that has been concealed,
or so we thought
until our thoughts proved us wrong
I don't mind readin' U,
but I love hearing you talk
Now we're reaching to new levels,
putting action to our thoughts
with our bodies, minds, and hearts
Right now I'm just thinkin'...
that our love is ART.

The Conversation Is Dope

Just wanted to hit you up, to tell you something
Another day is only promised if it's God willing
so if I hold back my feelings, it might be too late
If I keep them inside, I could make a mistake
Miss out on a blessing, by the actions I take
Don't mean to bring any confusion your way
but our conversations have me wondering if this is fate
Ever since our paths crossed, I've had this thought...
this thing in my heart connecting with who you are
and while I've tried to brush it off,
it comes back every time
Not to mention, our conversations are divine!
Dropping jewels all the time, whenever we speak
Building with peace of mind, you're not like everybody
It's just nice that I can be me
I'm glad you came into my life, whatever this all brings
So I don't know, I probably sound crazy...
but I'm thinking you're king enough to see
my sincerity when I tell you,
there is no need to fear with me
I'm that woman you can chill with any day
and be sure I won't cross you the wrong way
So if it's not too much to ask,
I think we should make the best of what we have
Have each other's backs,
share secrets and testimonies from the past
Live in the present
and only God knows what the future holds
but it might be a good idea
if we took initiative to keep things clear
when the conversation ends and
there is that brief moment

MS. TABU

when I think you could be my best friend
but then I think you might be my husband
and sometimes it seems like,
I'm the only one who knows it
I mean the conversation is dope,
but if you haven't noticed…
this bond we have has been anointed
Maybe I'll chill and never even show this
but it's inevitable that if I don't,
in assumption that there will be a tomorrow
then you might never know
and while the conversation will always be soulful,
I don't think the hesitation of us being close
is a good enough reason to let a chance go
You make me feel like a God-given poem
Think about it…
what if I never even wrote,
what a waste it would be
So basically...
if you pray to God and He says she is me,
just don't forget to move with your feet
instead of waiting around for a sign to read
When His light says "GO", I hope you won't be
misguided by these earthly streets
Distractions come from all directions
but there will never be,
a conversation too deep
to be interrupted
when the Holy Spirit speaks.

The Love Hummingbirds

Boy, you make me laugh
when I felt like crying
Don't ask why,
because I don't know
I'm just heartbroken
and it makes no sense
Honey, I know I'm a mess
Please don't judge me
in the middle of distress
I'm a diamond in the rough
until my dying day
I'm being buffed and shined
but some edges, just may stay

So baby, tell me can you love me
when the ice all breaks?
When I can't say, "Don't touch me!"
because my love creates
a beautiful earthquake
and it makes you shake
and it makes you take
my breath away
as your gravity escapes
into the core of
where our union was made
Tell me baby,
as each layer peels away
and you see every scar,
watching the way God
is healing my broken heart
Can you stand by my side
through a process this long?

I trust in God to accelerate me
above and beyond
all the things they did to me
And baby, I would always
treat you genuinely
Hurting you baby, isn't my style
If you treat me like a lady
and try to make me smile…
I think we can work this thing out!
No marriage can be perfect
but we can make the vows

Like Cherine Anderson
"You may not be a movie star,"
but boy, you have me
letting down my guards
every time you come around
Do you see it in my eyes?
I'm floating on clouds
but each time I jump to the next one,
I'm only drifting further away
from this expression
Can't find the words and it hurts
Every bubble of mine bursts,
it all becomes a blur
The wind is too strong
for these thoughts to survive
but I'm praying to God
to grow upon us grapevines
to make the most divine wine
that only ages and gets better with time

If you wrap around me,
I'm certain we'll become one
What exactly have you been running from?
You pop up occasionally
just to talk and drive me crazy,
analyzing reasons why...
Maybe I'm just not his type
Maybe five foot two point five
isn't his favorite height
Maybe he doesn't like the curvy silhouette
of my womanly design
Maybe he doesn't like a woman
with heart, soul, and mind
Maybe I'm just too shy
Tell me why I can get up on the Mic
in front of crowds of people
who at first glimpse criticize
and confidently deliver rhymes
that may change somebody's life
Tell me why, I can testify...
but boy, when it's just you and me,
I'm only full of butterflies
that hide behind flowers,
the kinds hummingbirds like
as they hymn a tune
I think you'd like
I think you'd like
And it goes like...
It goes like...

Dah Dah Deh Duh

Sweet lover,
thought I thought saw you
peeking through the window to my soul
Well darling, tell me what to call you
Think I forgot your name,
but I've still got my clothes
If you want to listen
to my funky rhythm flows
you should surely buckle,
this will be a wild ride
Sorry, I'm not being subtle
but I'm humble all the time
Glory goes to the one who beholds
this canvas of mine
If you need a hint, look up in the sky
You're something different
like lemonade in the wintertime
Well, I'd like a single cup
of the pink kind with ice
I don't mind a flavor
that stands out not quite right
See, my taste buds were orchestrated
by a composer so divine
that all I can do is play by these notes,
singing all the time...
Dah Dah Deh Duh
I don't mean to sound truant
like a runaway bride
I know when to submit,
I'll come to school if you like
Darling, you can teach me anytime
But right now I'd just like to fly kites

on an inappropriate day
Give each other valentines
on the wrong holiday
Be real fresh when the haters hate
and we imitate, in a silly mimic way
Dah Dah Deh Duh
Who on earth cares,
what they think of this poem?
I can drink the air, swim in a volcano
I can dance on ceilings, break the ordinary roles
We can climb a fence in the middle of division
Tell me, what's the consequence
of two people really living?
I caught you, secretly admiring
Found the love you wrote
in a locker deep inside
Now you want my combination
but you won't tell me why
Is the slot not good enough
for you to reach my mind?
Are you curious of
the contents hidden behind
Did you hear it through the girl talk line
that I'm with some other guy?
You want to see if his picture
is beside the mirror of my heart
But you need to dream bigger,
don't you buy into those thoughts
Then you wonder why
every time you call,
I don't pick up to talk
All you hear is my phone ring like...

Dah Dah Deh Duh
But I like your voicemails, sugar
Promise I've listened, to every one
Lately I'm just a busy woman...
full-time classes, music, performing and such
I know you want me live and unplugged
You're tired of loving me oh so distant
Well, why don't you come over for Thanksgiving?
Meet my sister and some friends...
a little fellowship, are you in?
I can cook up something sweet,
the kind of pie you like
and maybe if you married me,
you could fulfill every fantasy of your mind
But for now, you must control the lust
I don't want to slip and slide
on a downward spiral,
although it's tempting sometimes
Especially when you're nice
like romantic candle lights
You set the mood, it's true
Makes me want to do
bad girl things like...
Dah Dah Deh Duh.

If You Like It, I Love It

I'm having trouble paying attention
in this class we call life
'cause baby we've been passing notes
back-and-forth for some time
behind their backs like they can't see us
Sooner or later we will slip up
get caught with our love notes
written in body language
with felt-tip lips
as our double dipped kiss
travels back in time
to when quill pens were invented
This some 600 A.D. kind of chemistry
It could be problematic that there's no
principal suspending me
like Freshman days when I'd rather sleep
and make it to class late
but now I'd rather lace poetry
inspired by backaches
from all the bending back
we've been doing these days
Hiding in a secret place
knowing sooner or later
we're going to catch a case
of jealousy
when they find out the smile on my face
is helplessly
from being graced with your melody
expelling me from the courses
I never wanted to take, anyway
I'd rather sing with the band heaven plays
as we embrace the rhythm of our escapade

Daydreaming of what our song would be named
Maybe, *"If You Like It, I Love It"*,
who cares what they say?
This one will be a hit, I just know it!
Not the commercial tunes
that got played out
This some old school,
still hot when our grandchildren around
This that, Chico DeBarge, "No Guarantees"
on some *Long Time No See*
or that Raphael Saadiq,
"Ask of You", his 95' biggest release
kind of joint that makes me think...
what is it you ask of me?
Must I be something more extraordinary
than the down for whatever woman
living spiritually free of restraints
with my against the grain mentality
painting from my own palette, see...
all these rules were made to be broken
if they are to stop me from being next to you
I will be that bad girl if it means being true
to the proof in the pie, baby take a slice
and if you like it, I love it
with every bite.

Soul Love

Excuse me,
Am I being too forward?
Should I fall back?
Should I push more?
Whether or not I tug our love,
I'm feeling sore
Wounded without the war
But then it feels so good
because it hurts in those places
you caressed in the storm
when the rain poured
and the lightning flashed
in the living room
as passion was igniting at a latitude,
captivating us to getting struck inside
Would have thought I was
dripping with metal
from every crevice exposed
head to toes, curling remorseless
Nails to spine like thorns of roses
Flipping my body in ancient poses
Kama Sutra clouds raining down
Taste a hint of salt when I kiss your neck
Mouth open as we slow dance, getting wet
Puddles of sweat formulating in the bed
Nobody's home, we're just waiting for friends
Gracefully moaning from a pain this passionate
Pleasing me in ways past never knew to exist
Lathering in our natural oils
like we're roots in the soil
planted on each other's paths,
destined to intertwine

Tangling in the sign of sixty-nine
Harvesting the fruition of our design
Perfection aligned for the first time
Growing with you, while you're growing in me
Connecting our temples as oneness, infinitely
Never felt the hands of eternity
until I felt your hands working me
Lips whispering, word smithin' me
Nibbling at my tender sweets
Prints of cheeks covering the sheets
Betraying pillows with lustful teeth,
silencing me like Pussy Willows
around a rivers creek
Breathing strong like squall wind
as I stream rapidly between thighs
while you float on my visual paradise
like lily pads letting go of gravity,
trusting natures grasp
with no need to ask if it's the best we've had
Finally the climax leads us to relax
like an old soul brother playing the sax
So can you blame me for feeling that?
Pardon my inability to reel in that
unwinding emotion, revealing maps
that will lead you to every treasure
a real woman has.

Tabu Sutra

They say it's devilish
for him to kiss my crevices
but it feels like heaven opening gates,
when his taste buds trace my sacred vase
All knowledge of sin evacuates,
fast as intimacy enters
Could it be the many complexities
of this messenger
sent to deliver me simply pleasure?
Hooks me like garters
to the immaculate architecture
of his leaver
as he moves me
in directions astrological charts can't predict,
satellites can't trace
He wears Cupid's darts like a Bob Marley chain
Brings me to a place
where give or take
embodies one familiar face
Have I seen you somewhere before?
He be Déjà Vu me, "I had the craziest dream last night,"
manifested through chakras, destiny fully dilated
protesting like lava against the human race
many attempts to change nature
He is the vent for my vapor,
the pen to my paper,
the Zen of my favorite tea
The explanation for my intuition missing a beat
when my third eye blinked
and he'll always know the reason why,
Sade's "The Moon and the Sky"
is the theme of our vibe...

"Ain't going let you go",.
beyond the physical flesh
Love is always love on a level of spirit
His aura danced with me between sheets of soul
until mine transformed into a pink and white glow
upon his shadows black canvas
Kind of love make a white woman vanish to another planet,
come back a black pantheress,
fighting for my right to move to the front of his heart
Maybe next lifetime will come early
Rolls me like dice with uncertainty
yet somehow a higher "entity" has churned the cream
into a milky stream we follow subconsciously
Shooting stars we are, lost but with a cause
Mastered Kama Sutra like a walk in the park
yet amateurs to the words our mouths don't talk…
"What spark?" Egos object,
while the sequel connects, connects, connects…
are we there yet?

Crazy Obsession

I know you've had other women tell you a tall tale
They said they would cross the ocean, put up the sail
They said you would never drown by their side
But tell me why I found you at the bottom
with no life in your eyes?
Now you ask me, what made me carry you to the top?
Lie your body on the shore of my heart, give you CPR
Synchronizing mine with yours just to feel your beat
Ever since the first time I felt you inside me
I've had a crazy obsession
with you spending your life with me
I don't know what you think, but I know the deal
I caught you looking at engagement rings,
when you thought I was asleep still
Should they call me insane when I am looking so crazy?
Forgetting where I parked and looking frantically
for my keys while I'm out shopping for groceries
Every time you call I am ready to run
Doesn't matter who I'm with or where I'm at
As long as I'm not in the middle of performing,
I've got your back
As long as I don't forget about my girls
just to put you on my map
Tell me, can I have more than sweet memories
to hold onto when the nights are cold?
Can we live for right now,
through the windows of our soul?
Can you see all the things I never say?
Maybe I'm just afraid of all the games guys play
Maybe I need a man to help lead me the right way
Now don't trip, the Lord is right here with me
I just need a man to love and support me

I just need my feet rubbed after a show
and maybe you can run that bathwater for me
Maybe you can lather my body with something sweet
Baby, can you do that for me or am I completely out of line?
My mind is on the grind just trying to find ways I can
hustle this love to work for us in a way that will be legitimate
I see all these haters trying to burn us up,
throw us in the fire like we ain't nothing but dust
but my obsessions so crazy that it fireproofed us
They ain't got the weapon to stop this crazy obsession
They keep on pressing but I cut them like a C-section
Deliver them from my belly and stitch up my skin
I won't be carrying those demons for their own sins
Never knew how amazing a crazy obsession could be
It feels like the type of protection that is always for keeps
I expect nothing but the unexpected but I need you to love me
Tell me, are you the guard of my heart or am I just a prisoner?
I can't tell the difference anymore
if I'm missing the big picture
when my mind is oriented around the details
of those little things you do…
how you smell my hair, watch me sleep,
and make love on love's throne, under the morning glow
There isn't a carpet red enough to show how royal
this crazy obsession makes me feel
Feeding me grapes in the bed like you're for real
so whether this will be a blessing or a lesson
all that I can say is, it was nothing less than
a crazy obsession.

Our Love Is Funky

He makes me spill like mad milk...
so nonchalantly dips his chocolate chip soul
in my thoughts not distilled
He be like, "Be still!"
While he reads me like fine print on a contract,
selling your life to a record label
And he be spinning me like tracks,
he just knows the way they go
like the lyrics of my heart be written in his soul
no... be written in his poems
He picked me like a rose that stood out special...
petals a little more full,
colors vibrant enough to move him
on the dancefloor
He got me tripping like a disco ball,
hanging in places I never did before...
looking like silver rainbows in a crowd of dark clouds
He sips my aura like juicy mango's in some island town
Mixes me up like a Piña Colada
and convinces me that I'm the showstopper,
the queen of water, the sacred spring,
the shining diamond in the projects
that makes the mute man sing
He practices me like religion...
bathes in me like being christened,
pours me like anointing oil all over him
says he feels blessed like a sunken ship saved
He likes to play chess but he don't like to run game,
he just wishes that I would check my mate...
that I would get my fair play or rather play fair
says he don't like to chase, but he will see me there.

Love for Love

He drank my love in the rain
dancing with the rain drops of my heart
bathing in the chemical reactions to my... pain
in between that place where joy is in arm's reach
He wondered if she'd reach or if she'd keep
distantly practicing their symphony,
making a solo act of their duet
Was she playing Russian roulette with his emotions?
Did she even know it?
How that one bullet,
could go through the head of their love
and there it would lay
growing new life through its buds
Should have been dead but never was
She tells him she needs to leave,
she needs to go
and he never quite seems
to get out the words, "Don't!"
Gone too fast, too soon
but he knows she'll be back
because she comes with the moon
So let her flirt with the sun,
sharpen her shine on the rays of its love
only to have a sharper blade when it cuts
into his wound where she planted their "us",
Cleansing the infection
of the world that left it neglected
but it seems she thinks, she is the disease
when she is the reflection of the cure
He thinks...
"Soon my star will see,
she was birthed pure!"

So he protects the seeds she left for him to secure
although she never gave instructions, she didn't have to
because it was written in the way she loved him,
that gave him the map to all the ways of their love for love
He nurtured the pieces of her like they were, pieces of him
because they were each a piece of his rib
and she was, his woman
Her ego tells her she can't stand him
but the irony is that she is still standing
in the melted shadow of their last embrace,
looking like a candle with its wick out of place
and every time she thinks she's gone without a trace,
she forgets that he beholds her ambiance in a safe
locked between their spirits that pray
for the day to come when she willfully opens
to the tranquility of a love for love, God-chosen
It's a funny joke really, the kind nobody laughs at
because nobody seems to get the irony of their past that
presented itself in the presence of their hands that dwelt
in the remains of silly stories,
telling all the ways they'd met before
as their auras giggled in playful colors, dipping in each other's,
blending together as one, as "new" gets rediscovered.

Dreaming of You

Anointed by the tenderness of your patience
Infatuation would be an understatement
Don't know what keeps me, keeping you waiting
knowing I'm more than just the subject of paintings
but still I hide out in an internal basement
even when there is no storm
Never forgotten,
how you covered me when there was
My dear, never feel that your umbrella
was never enough
Never think that opening it inside of my soul
where you found home, was bad luck
Know that gently tugging at the petals of my heart
didn't end on "She loves me... not."
Still, you never picked them off
You only nurtured my inner flower with your love
Letting nature be, fully appreciating me
at every phase of growth
even when the thorns came
and I lost hope,
you knew my season would come
as you seasoned me with what you knew I was made of…
Passionate Love
Reminding me of the ancient roots that birthed me here
Knowing my pain didn't always come in the form of tears
You hugged my soul at times when I didn't even know
how badly I needed it until feeling you close
Whispering sweet sunflower secrets to me
in the form of a poem
Driving yourself mad with the inability to guard me
from all that may harm me
but trusting our creator to walk me

through burning flames
even when it burned you inside
Wishing to wear every scar of mine on your own skin
just to honor the battlefield that made me stronger than
a pair of secret lovers lips sealed in tribal times
or in the days of "black and white", but wait...
it seems as though we're still living those, sometimes
Still, you'd stand with me in front of all who oppose,
get down on your knees and propose
even if they shot you down saying, "I love you," in the road
Knowing this love was bullet proof,
vested by divine truths and a God who
lets no weapon prosper against those who,
live according to His rules
which overrule the imaginary need to follow
packs of people who say what we "should" do
based on artificial reasons like skin pigmentation,
social status, and disbelieving that true love exists
beyond limitations set by conditioned beings
All it takes is visions of your heart beating
for me to survive moments of suffocation
in a place where oxygen is taken
and replaced with immediate gratification
Where soul trading is the common expectation
You remind me of the little things I find amazing
no matter the situation
and you look at me as if you see
these desert butterflies fluttering in my belly,
gracefully embracing the heat that has formed
between you and me king
So even though I've yet to make this
a you-and-me thing in my physical shell

It seems my spirit begs to differ on a higher level
where mistakes do not exist
when guided by perfect alignment
of a love designed with the inability to tell time
So I'm sorry if you feel like
I'm hitting the snooze button
one thousand times over on this love
but just know that I was
dreaming
of you.

I Can't Breathe

Sometimes it feels like I can't breathe
Like I'm stuck inside of my dreams
Subconsciously living scenes of you and me
Swear my heart skips a beat
every time you steal my breath from me
I remember the first day I saw you
Talk about it
I played hard, like I'd never call you
and now your number, *I'd be lost without it*
People say I'm tripping, I'm sweating
They say I'm just missing the affections
Is the ice princess melting all over again?
I don't want to say it's different than other men
Truthfully, I don't even want to think of them
what's done is done, old love is gone
If I show my emotions, don't get me wrong
This is more than just a song,
more than a poem whether it's hot or not
Am I allowed to be human for a minute?
Can I just say I'm at my limit?
I don't want to be hurt again
I don't want to give a chance
nor do I want to miss a blessing
See, breathing used to be second nature
but being around you makes me think
about each breath I take here,
living on borrowed time
Knowing that before I die,
I want a child with my eyes
with your smile, with my lips
with our hair, a combination
and a beautiful twist, of our skin

She can carry our legend,
harvest seeds in our garden
while we endure love eternally
The day will come when
you and me can no longer breathe
So every breath I take,
I make sure I breathe deep but
Sometimes it feels like I can't breathe
like I'm stuck inside of my dreams
Sub-consciously living scenes of you and me
Swear my heart skips a beat
every time you steal my breath from me
Sometimes I just want you here with me
Simplicity is really the key to please me
I'm a complex lady, I need some lightweight things
I need relaxation, massages between sheets
Your fascination with the message in my poetry
It's like… you understand the language of me
You translate me perfectly
You say you even hear my voice as you read
and I think that's kind of deep
like I know just what you mean
because I hear your voice every time I breathe
Every time my soul screams, "Just love me please!"
Secretly I cry, "Don't hurt me, just set me free!"
I don't mean to get bitter from time-to-time
when I'm angry with the lack of real love in this life
Usually men my age don't have mature minds
So the age difference, I no longer mind
I take it for what it is
I'm an old soul with a gift to consistently grow
Even when I can't breathe somehow God accelerates me

I'm right where I was ordered to be
So if you're stepping with me it's okay to take the lead
as long as we ain't going to fire pits
I've come too far, to go backwards on bliss
That's why I said,
God must be the center of our relationship
The rock in between our hard place
Sometimes it will be hard
going through these healing days
Sometimes we might argue,
sometimes we might cry
but there is nothing God can't do
if we trust him each time
to let our love within vaporize
Sometimes it feels like I can't breathe
like I'm stuck inside of my dreams
Subconsciously living scenes of you and me
Swear my heart skips a beat
every time you steal my breath from me
Sometimes we fight over stupid things
Sometimes it's just an artist thing,
deciphering the difference between
our expressions and realities
If I wear an outfit you find too sexy
If that skit you did makes me sketchy
Somehow we get distracted
but then, you be joke cracking
I be laughing, we back again
Plus you love me when I'm broke,
or bringing in profit
Living gig-to-gig,
or a nine-to-five grind that feels robotic

And with that said...
Sometimes it feels like I can't breathe
like I'm stuck inside of my dreams
Subconsciously living scenes of you and me
Swear my heart skips a beat
every time you steal my breath from me.

He and I

I wrote a poem…
about how the moon became full when we kissed
painting our tongues iridescent shades
in hues of silvers, grays, and blues
Even my irises reflected this artists palette
flowing down a river, he held me breathless
He speaks as if he is the Canute
that delivered the emergency message
to my heart in a bottle opened with no cork
He wonders why I don't remember him
when he was the one who loved me more
than the others who left me there, torn
He writes poetry like he wants to give me my firstborn
He births his ink into me like he enjoys me pregnant, sore
He writes poetry that makes my heart beat, grow,
and leak into his soul
to feed his spirit that teethes on my woman-being
He writes poetry that sings lullabies to my future maternity
When he writes, my ears ring
I hear him, piercing my dreams
with the rhythm of his pencil, sharpening itself on me
as I try to digest the chips that shed in my chest, pieces of him
He writes like, these are pieces of me
He writes like these were ancestry dreams
that came to him in his sleep, told him where he would find me
somewhere in between destiny and the eternal trees
He lyrically, metaphorically,
poetically ravages me between his sheets…
loose-leaf, says he would have writer's block
if he ever were to lose me
So I wrote a poem to tell him I was sorry
for losing my glass slipper at his doorstep

with a poem folded up in the sole that expressed
my secrets about the poems he wrote, feelings I've never said
I should have been more careful when we're both romantics
I knew he'd come searching for me to take my foot in his palm
after this feeling of urgency
made me run to my hiding spot, a pool of stars
but he knows where I write my poems
So I wrote a poem about how, it was just a poem
These were all just... "poems"
and for a moment...
as my feet bathed with the stars, tickling my toes...
this just a poem, poem was believable
until suddenly my eyes were covered with silk blindfolds
and I felt a wordsmith's hands around my ankles
as he began to read the poem, I swore I'd never wrote
but it was impossible to deny being responsible
for the tears that dripped from his eyes onto my skin
as he recited, over and over again until I finally did admit
that this was indeed the poem about his poems I wrote for him
This was the page that never made it into my book
This was the space that made him say,
"Something is missing," when he got to that chapter
For once he wanted me to feel
without seeing things that didn't matter
He wanted to be real in my world
without merely living off the echo of my laughter
He said those girlish giggles
kept him breathing all year long
but that he's let them go like fireflies
that stopped glowing in the dark
and now has come to tell me, that he wrote a poem
about how lucky some men are...

to have had the chance to hold the woman
with the most, beautiful broken heart
and how he'd give up everything
to have had a chance to break it too
just so that he could be the one who doesn't
so I took off the blindfold to look deep into his soul
and I told him, that I know these poems were never poems
but that he could write on me, with me,
in me, through me, into me for all his days to come
if he promises, that these will never be just poems to us
that I will never be just a scroll
sticking out from his back pocket,
that I will never be something he memorized
hoping that lines would not be forgotten,
that he would never forget to tell me
the lines he'd never written
I needed to know him beyond his imagination
I needed to be more than the poetess
who had him in captivation
I needed to do more than rhyme
the right way in the right stanza, at the right time
I needed him to love me
even during times when it's more difficult to write
Even if others may try to plagiarize precious lyrics
shared between you and me
I need you to know, nobody can do it quite like us
that our copyrights exist in the heaven's above
that it's not about what flows off the tips of these poets tongues
it's about what we feel within
and we're feeling love for love
So then we wrote a poem together as one
with our only writing instruments, being us.

He's My Orchard

His love warms me like a fine cup of apple cider
I like walking through the orchards of his mind
picking fresh fruits
he says, "Take any kind you like,"
and I like them all…
but I don't get gluttonous on a brother
I've got fruits of my own
Mutually we offer a fair trade of
"flesh of his flesh, bone of his bone"
and he says he digs the pumpkin pie of my soul
He says the way my eyes change colors
Reminds him of home sweet home
where the leaves fall and turn over
in hues that blend so beautiful
He's something sweet like the smell
of autumn wind in crisp breeze
carefully reminding me that
love's seasons may change
With winter around the corner,
I need a man to keep me safe
Warm my bodies vase,
be my dark hot chocolate on a windy day
Whip the cream of me spiritually,
and soften me like marshmallows
when autumn keeps teasing me,
telling me it's about to snow
then unbelievably,
your presence manifests reflections
of conceiving seeds,
toasting them in an oven called eternity,
carving happy faces in the skin of me

Reminding me,
"Baby be patient, when it's true love found."
So I snuggle inside of our cocoon
where you cuddle with my light
like it's your favorite truth
Wrapping it around the safety we seclude
from a world better known as "World War II"
and in one trillion shades
of orange, yellow, golden, and brown
you tell me, "I am FALL… ing in love with you,"
as my canvas answers, whispering…
"Darling, we are never stagnant caterpillars,
our wings shall soon spread as we break loose,
you are my husband and the fragile scales
of my design were made for you
so cherish each color, each dot, each line
and know that for every man,
there harvests one butterfly."

Let's Make Dreams

I told him
if he poured his dreams on me
that I would bathe in them
let them soak into my skin
Pouring my dreams
into the same tub,
I'd invite him to come in.

I said, that if he shampooed my hair
with the whispers of every wish he ever made
that I would feel beautiful to be there
in this mixture of stars, pennies, prayer
and I would stay

If he wanted me to,
I would squeeze every last drop of sugar
from the sweet tooth of my soul
into his mouth to soothe his throat...

I'd get my angel wings wet
in his essence if it meant
that we could do this again and again
and if he promised to dry them
when we were finished
but only if he would keep me warm
with the heat that oozes
down his spine
whenever his chemistry
morphs into mine
Only if he would dance with me
through a field of our childhood
that we could make believe we met back then

Rewrite our life storybook
We could share our first kiss,
one for each year
Time travel through innocence
and fast forward past tears

If we could just be happy, right here
wherever we are
then I would open every single jar
and let the butterflies in my belly
fly free at last

If he could walk with me
through a jungle of broken dreams
and rescue them with me
If he could be brave when I'm scared
and strong when I'm weak
but then change roles whenever we need

I told him, to just believe...
Scrub away all of our insecurities
Blend all his layers into me, like one tree
Grow with me

I said that I'd let him swim through my eyes
if he'd let me dive into his beneath the moon
Let our spirits learn, guide, caress each other
while we cleanse together, our minds
and connect the eternity of two lovers
I told him I'd break each hourglass open
Let the salt grains disintegrate in our bath
and show him that time no longer knows when

If him and I could hold hands, become timeless
and let God control the hour rather than man

I told him…
it's time to dream again
Do you remember when?
It used to be so easy then.
The way we were, so free
with our imaginations
What happened?
Shh… I understand.

Drink from my passion, savor it
Let it bring back the moments
when dreams would vapor from within
Be comforted,
by the softest skin of a woman
who loves you without conditions
There are no limits…
What horizons?

Just fly
like we've nowhere to go
Swing high from your favorite
branch of my soul
Call me your home sweet home
Wear me like heaven
were tattooed on your skin
Sink deep into me, like an ocean
all the way to the bottom
to find my mysteries
and treasures, hidden

Have your way with me,
whichever way that may be
One body floating
in a sea of purity
Run away with me
Marry me
behind the waterfalls
of our dreams

Lie with me in a bed
of living flowers
and bloom beautifully
Kiss the stars that drip
from my tear ducts
and call me, "Love."

Be my love hummingbird
Land on me gently,
silently tasting the pollen of me
for which you yearn
Give me fever just to make me better
Increase the temperature
until our candle burns,
melting into each other
Wishing, dreaming,
loving on one another

Give me therapy, heal me
as God tells you, "It's her."
It's me,
the woman of your dreams
The never-ending inkwell of poetry

Pour into me like liquid pennies
Manifest into gold
Empty every dream, every wish,
just let them go

Call me your dreamcatcher,
crafted just for you
Always remember
that dreams come true
For you dreamed of me
and I dreamed of you

Now let's make dreams,
never forgotten
Keep dreaming with me,
forever lost in
the dream we fall in
when love is
our only
inspiration.

If I Could Just

If I could just...
take a day to lie with you in bed
and worry about nothing
Melt away into nothingness with you,
letting go of everything
If I could just listen to your heartbeat for awhile
without you having to ask me what I'm thinking about
Just be. Just quietly cherish these moments of peace
Turn our phones off, don't want to be bothered anymore
If I could just live inside your love
and forget about external war
Just... take my clothes off and not have to worry about
explaining why I'm naked when my spirit fits me perfect
Just stop worrying, stop hurting,
stop murdering faith with fear
Stop being nervous to take it here with you
Stop assuming what you might do if I do
Just do. Do what I feel, free from "think"
If I could just heal each time you touch me,
and in my scars, you could see my beauty
because you see nothing scarred about me
If I could just trust the fact that
this is exactly where I'm supposed to be on my path
that you are him and I am she
and we were meant to be
If I could just ask you to marry me
without sounding completely crazy
and you could propose to me
before we even have the rings
If we could do it the way it was supposed to be
regardless of where we stand financially, start a family
If we could just have a chance to be alive

I curl up next to your body and begin to cry
You don't ask why because you understand,
living in this society is like being scammed
If we could just breathe for a bit,
enjoy the simplicity of our existence
Another kiss is never promised
when another day of life isn't
So if we can just kiss until the sun rises
If I can just fall into your arms
when I'm too tired to walk anymore,
too tired to stand alone,
too sore to crawl
Just give me a day where I don't need to be strong
Just let me be weak without risking it all
Just give you my heart to restore
Just let down my guards, protected by yours
Put all my projects on pause,
just be adored.

Good Morning, Love!

This morning,
I opened my eyes
with the vibration of your
three a.m. whispers
resonating inside
Vague memories from my
subconscious mind,
prompting my heart
to speak through
a rhythm of beats
that simply mean...
"I love you too,"
as he tightens his
strong arms
around my midline
This is how we slept
last night
The lovers lock,
about to be the lovers rock
My body anticipating
how his will respond
to subtle motions of approval
for him to worship at my altar
in any way he likes
Full submission
to his deepest desire
has his sensory
in overdrive
over my
touch
Doing everything I can
to make my man

feel loved and cared for
with special treatment
Paying attention
to what makes every hair
on his body stand
so I can do it again and again
Steadily giving the utmost pleasure
Falling more in love with him
every morning we're together
Never too tired, take me as I am
I'm coming correct,
with no excuses why we can't
Twenty-four seven
unlimited supply of passion
Multiple ways to express it
but right now I'm focused on
between these sheets action
in its essence
Never undermine
something designed
by the most divine
to reconnect a man to his wife
Free from the pain this world brings
in a zone where all is lost
except for two
found in sync as one
Yes, this is the definition of making love
and simply how we say,
"Good Morning, Love!"

Greedy

If it were up to me I'd be so "greedy"
One million lifetimes together would be
a bare minimum
I'd max out that diva card
to the limits in a minute
just to make sure I'm the queen of your heart
I sound so crazy, but you like it
I tell you... one life is, too short
If I had ten extra hearts,
I'd give them all to you before
you even had the nerve to ask
In full armor I'd fight the deadliest of wars,
just to win you back
Rest assured, you'd have been my
first and last in every future
and past we had
My body would know no other hands
Lips wouldn't kiss no other man
Mind would have no recollection
of any lover before we met when
your spirit called my name
in a dialect ingrained in my DNA
as we played a game of
philosophizing higher understandings
Friend-zoning for years
until we finally lost our hand in,
hiding from this love
I like this love,
I like it so much
that I'd freeze the world in place
just to race into your arms one millisecond faster

I'd put my two weeks' notice in
just so we could sleep mornings in
without having to leave your side
but I'll be late to work, just to kiss you goodbye
I'd play every lottery ticket there is
hoping we'd win, just for the chance
to put this glass ceiling beneath us
so we could be us, without these
superficial routines to which we succumb
Frankly, I view the world as an interruption
and if it were up to me…
I'd rip open every seam
on the all American dream,
find the way out of this scene
just for seven minutes
of you alone with me
in our bittersweet reality
but I'd be so greedy…
I'd need another forever
in eternity,
for each lifetime I'm with you.

When It's Love

He asked me,
"How do you know when it's love?"
I answered, love...
in every form
has one origin,
one source
and like its creator
is timeless
No beginning
No end
Just is
Don't be confused...
Sure you and I
in the physical sense
began when we met
at a place in time
we remember well
But in the spiritual realm
this, darling always been
Before the lovemaking
Before the first dates,
I lied to myself saying weren't dates
Before the "shacking up",
making babies,
tying the knot
Doing some,
backwards love dance
folks couldn't quite
catch the rhythm of
This love still soared
through the heavens,

no boundaries,
unconditional
with a wingspan
that never faced limits
of the sky and earth
Free to stretch out
Free to grow
fly
fall,
do whatever it may
So darling...
I know it's love
by the scent of eternity
our passion brings
anywhere we land
Gravity cannot contain
the transcendence of our love
Crowded rooms cannot lose it in the mix
Traffic jams can't cease its flow
Pollution is no threat to this love,
breathing pure life into our being
For we are but one
divided into two bodies;
Man and Woman,
connected spiritually
The epitome of oneness
Street lights can't stop it
Nothing man-made can
touch
tame
burn

break
or even build,
this love
No see, the potter responsible
for something so divine
has molded this love
with His own hands
leaving it firm enough to
be steadfast
Soft enough to morph
change
transition
the way He sees fit
This thing ain't even
our doing you see
So while we're thinking
I chose him... her
He chose us,
for this love
So I say…
you know when it's love
when time holds power no more
When, "How did you meet?"
can only truly be answered
by souls that just seem
to glide through the moments
and memories that bring
sentiment everlasting
It's like we're just...
stepping in footprints already there,
hence déjà vu

That feeling like this love was already there
and we are simply arriving
to our destiny awaiting
no matter how long it takes
Always there
Always been
Always will be
No matter how far off track
we think we've gone
This love lights the way
Not back
Not forth
Just... the way
and like that good old North Star,
we follow it home.

Real Love Is Back in Style

Drift away with me sweet love
to a place where we can be us
where it doesn't matter,
the way people see us for everything we're not
and miss the whole point of who we are
"The Point of It all",
turn on the Anthony Hamilton and steal my heart
Stay for a while, make yourself at home
Real love is coming back in style
and I'm the trend-setter of this brand called 'Eternal'
Let me upgrade you dear
Give you a makeover right here
Oh sugar, I will kiss away your tears
Tell me gentleman, what did she do?
If you can, please tell me the truth
Did she emotionally cripple you?
Did she use you and abuse you?
So you let down your guards
only for her to break your heart
but you can't miss out on real love
because of something you've been through once
Look at me babe, what do you think?
Do I seem like a lady who's never been through a thing?
Well my king, you are mistaken and I'll tell you why…
I've been through all types of situations with guys
See my life has been rough
and if you can't handle my scars
If it's all too much to know my flaws
If you're just another man to miss the point of it all
then what's the point of being here at all?
You can go if you'd like but darling, please know
I'm the kind of lady a real man will make his wife

Yes, my chance will come to walk down the aisle
and meet my real love there at the altar where he awaits
Tears flowing like water and the look on his face,
he saw the most beautiful woman
and knows no one could take her place
so my hand he takes
Forever and always he will stay
I hope this doesn't scare you away,
but I've learned the hardest way through broken hearts
that I cannot change for the worse
to keep a man around based on his pace
I will always accelerate beyond expectations people make
If we can do it in six months, then we can do it today
Love is more than just an emotion, it's a choice
Part of me is hoping you feel this inner voice
speaking loud and clear
that you've found a woman so sincere
You had better treat her like
you don't want to lose her and fear
that you will if you don't let your feelings show
Sweet love, I have to let you know…
it's time to put those lovers in the past
if we want to move forward to the plans God has
Look, I get it...
you had it bad for a woman who had it good
You did everything you could just to make it work
but the point of it all is you were
with the wrong woman even if she looked good
Wouldn't you rather spend your life with a lady
who is pretty, sweet, and has goals all the time?
A lady who is spiritual, loves God first, lives a prayer life,
and needs a man to pray with her on nights like tonight

Take my hands baby, Shh… it's okay
Don't push me away, let's pray
Bet you never had a woman care enough
to keep you safe in the arms of the Lord
Bet when she breaks your heart,
she isn't sorry for making it harder for
the good girl trying to make you see…
every other woman in this world, is not me
I am not she,
and we'll never be comparatively, adjacent
So take your time with me
but don't let time be wasted
Real love is a chance and you have to take it
Who knows when it will come again?
This might just be it.
Let me show you how a real woman
makes you smile
The things she's supposed to do
Babe, you're living in denial
Real love is back in style as of right now!
A man wasn't made to be alone
So let me know what your plans are
and bring us home
Tired of renting out my soul to men
who will never invest in
keeping me as their own
Aren't you done being sold out
on just the physical?
Isn't it time to seek
the inside of a woman and grow?
Build an emperor of real love
and be seated on a throne

Aren't you tired of having nobody to hold?
I know I'm tired of writing these poems
about what I want but don't have so…
if this is real love, let it show and don't never let it stop
Yes love, real love is coming back in style
so tell everyone you know…
that it comes in every color, every size, and fits "unconditional"
Real love has no limits unlike that bootlegged ghetto show
folks thought was the real thing but now you know…
that if it isn't real love, then it isn't valuable
I'm putting that other stuff out of business
so either get with real love or be the laughingstock
of the real love era,
back from lifetimes ago.

Love Is...

Love is foot massages when her shift ends
learning reflexology only to use it for them
It's desiring to heal him, take the pressure off
knowing they've been on their legs all day
overworked, underpaid, it's...
riding for you when skies are grayest.

Love is praying, against every stronghold, curse, temptation
before they leave in the morning and on their way home
Love is me, writing this poem
Love is baking their favorite meal...
nurturing the body with herbs to calm the soul

Love is I will, I do, and I won't
ever betray you or disobey vows we spoke
when we know, the power words between us and God hold.

Love is freedom from the oppression of un-love,
from obsession disguised as right love
Love doesn't hide from us, love is all cards upfront -
"This is what it is, this is who I am
understand, the complexities and flaws,
pros and cons before you be my man."

Love is, pulling you from the quicksand,
"Here love, let me give you a hand."
Love is no such thing as "we can't", when we can
Love is, connecting, expressing, and dissecting
what's preventing our paths from meeting again.

Love is again, and again, and again.
Love is my lover, my teammate, my friend.

Love is not merely tying the knot, but building on,
all the reasons you tied it in the first place
Love is, first place

Love is remembering anniversaries and birthdays
while never forgetting to make them feel special on all days
Love is always, even when you've, "Had it up to here!"
Love is the clear road for safe travels
when others haven't been plowed yet

Love is the queen of yoga, mastering new positions
to bend in without ever breaking
Love is a seed making its way through spiritual realms,
ready to be nurtured by elements we possess

Love, doesn't hurt her, or mess with her head
Love is quite the opposite;
so many impostors have tried mocking it
but see the difference is… love don't quit

I know what love is from the moment I saw it…
that old man helping his queen to her feet,
loving her despite the way time had taken its toll

Love is beautiful!
I want to look like love, be like love, and speak like love
I want that to be like us, one day.

When Dreams Become Realities

I have had many sweet dreams that never came true
Waking up disappointed as I lay in my reality
I've lived nightmares in conscious episodes of my life
where pools of sweat soaked up my mind
I've seen friends give life and I've seen friends die
but I never knew the kind of reality
that becomes the sweetest dream
Falling asleep in deep pleasure
Wallowing in being happy, how could this be?
Did you know this is what I dreamed of since I was a little girl?
Back when I used to walk around like a little lady
saying how I was never getting married
and would forever stay with Daddy
Eventually I gave up being the independent bag lady
for the fantasy of being loved
Mommy always used to say I had stars in my eyes
Well, she must have known my heart cried
with a glitter that would mesmerize
She must have known there would be guys
to try to squeeze my sparkle until I couldn't shine
You see as a young teen all I knew of love
suddenly was butchered in the gutter
where there was no more pulse
So you want to know why I'm so scared,
still looking for the monster in the closet
when there's nothing there
Still waiting for him to become one of them
when I know he is sincere
but I'm making excuses for my fears
I hope I'm enough but not too much
I fear the itch of my impatience
and my temptation to scratch it

until it bleeds away the language of our hearts
and we can't speak the native tongue
of our origin anymore,
losing the accent that made everyone sure
of our foreign identity
as we remained secure in a society
that imprisons true love
like the enemy in this reality TV culture
where asking someone to love you for who you are is like…
asking them to sacrifice identity on their ego cards
Where the right amount of money
is enough to buy your heart
and selling soul is not only normal, but expected
I'm scared to take it slow
when tomorrow might be breathless
I need the brave little girl in me
because this grown woman is too used to
the heart aching sting it can bring
Baby, I don't want to feel anymore
if feeling means you would leave me
when less looks like more
The grass isn't greener on the other side…
it's just painted for trickery to hypnotize us to roll the dice
I just want to be the kind of woman your momma likes
when she envisions the woman you should marry
I just want my Daddy to be proud this time
if I finally have a man who will ask him for my hand
I just need to build a family
with someone who understands me as I do him
I've got a sweet tooth for love and affection
Tell me, will you be the one quenching?
Will you be the satisfaction to my legacy?

I know it may seem scary, but I'm down for the ride
For every time life goes down, there will be a rise
Should we hold on tight or let our hands free?
I will follow if you will lead
Try my best to trust you to trust in me
I know that I can love you, can you love me?
Let's not waste our energy missing opportunities
while searching for pleasant trees
instead of staying with the one that will grow strong
Weathering through every storm just to earn the sunshine
warming its branches like arms
If you and me were the trunk of a tree,
tell me how many rings could there be?
Would you spend a lifetime with a woman like me?
We've got a lot to learn, so why don't we take a seat?
If you're ready, plant your roots deeply next to me.

Seasons of Love

If your heart turned cold, I'd open my mouth
and wait... for the snowflakes on my tongue
I'd embrace the snowstorm of your soul
I'd spread my wings and make angels out of your,
beautiful, unpredictable, change of weather so...
baby don't you go, thinking I can't love you so
I would shovel away the way to your last hope
clean the gutters of your faith
sled down the hills that had you shamed
I understand that seasons can't stay the same
Some things need not be explained
Sweet love, honey taste…
the way you always erase the day
Drip your healing texture down walls of pain
Suddenly they soften, and break
like dabs of light in my darkest moment

You fill me up, keep me warm
ready for the rain to pour on our parade
Seasons never stay the same
but it makes us appreciate the sun rays
when it's all said and done babe
After slow dancing to rhythms of raging skies
and loving even when the melancholy strikes
You remind me I'm special
even when the weatherman ain't right
Through unexpected situations,
we've connected like two hands praying…
like oneness in the midst of segregation
So basically what I'm saying is…
whatever the temperature,
even when other times were better

I see the bigger picture,
the purpose in all things
So if you're hurting
there is no sense in drowning
just to make believe
I'd rather see every side of your being
to be certain I unconditionally
love every flaw and weakness
so that as we change, grow
we will have a foundation built
to run back to
when we need to remember...
what it was like that year in December

What got us here?
Where did we find strength?
How did we stay honest
when the truth could do damage?
Keep a promise when our word
was so hard to manage
How did we first fall?
Who made the first call?
Who was there by your side to fight this war
when winds tried to steer us wrong
and people tried to predict our love gone?
Spoke a curse on us
but we came back to the pond,
washed ourselves clean of every evil thought
Fell into each other's arms
thanking God for what He's done
After all, while we couldn't control the seasons
we could trust God to season us

with all the things needed
to keep this love beating
and it never skips as we live every moment
It's not perfect but it's worth every hardship
I can't pick out any part that wasn't wanted
and he feels the same...
no matter how
these seasons
change.

Must've Been Love

The rain kept falling, my heart kept calling
Felt like I could feel everything around me...
branches breaking, ants crawling
Mothers shouting to their children to get in
but all I wanted to hear was your voice
Standing there in the middle of the storm
morphing with the lightening, swarmed by orbs
Spirit angels, lifting me up to the skies
brought me to your window, watched you sleep tonight
Rock-a-bye baby, I wish I could come inside
but my will has betrayed me, maybe...
I don't know what's going on...
I'm on the treetop singing our song
Never meant to break your heart
All those times I couldn't hold on
Needed a man right here by my side
but I swear I will love you for life
even when the wind stops
there is nothing that can come between us
I heard these so-called preachers
telling me when it hurts too much to give it up
but there's something that keeps us
It must've been love, must've been
Must've been the first night we met in the flesh
Must've been the making out session that led to the bed
We'd been talking for a while, but this was quite different
Oh, blame it on the music, let Hip-Hop confess it
Knew just what she was doing, when she introduced him
I felt like a hummingbird moaning a soft melody
every time you nurtured your favorite flower
Must've been love that never let this go sour
The roots still come up each spring and summer

But sometimes, sometimes the winters get cold
Sometimes I think I'm falling in love with some other "Joe"
Ain't it crazy, all these years we never had a label
Still there is this sincerity to be honest about where we go
but I've found I only have one home
so if you see me acting crazy now, it's because I finally know
I'm sorry I'm going out of control
bombarding you when I'm so emotional
I just thought you should know
from the bottom most inner parts of my soul
that there ain't no love poem capable
of painting those master works of art
that made me keep brushing up against your heart
Must've been our sweet love
Must've been those feet rubs
Must've been the way we had the candles lit
Chico Debarge and Neosoul songs playing
All of that good eating and dinner conversation
All of these memories, couldn't be a hallucination
I'm not just seeing things, I know it's real
You told me you're in love with me and it made me feel
Pinched my arm but you were still here
You've tasted every part of me, even my tears
I feel like you've waited for me, for all these years
and if you're leaving me now...
I cannot bare to face all these dark clouds
following me around
You've always brought me the rainbow
even when the thunder was so loud
that I couldn't hear the colors pouring down
wrapping around us until the sun comes back out
You've been the calm to my storm whenever in doubt

Don't leave me like these acorns lying dead on the ground
Can't you see baby? I've got some new wings now
I'm ready to try them out
Won't you come out and play with me?
Waiting patiently, have you mistaken me?
Baby it's me, in another form!
I know you see me, in those dreams of yours
I'm not leaving anymore
I've learned the lesson all before
Must've been love that made me so sure
there's got to be a standing chance
I know we've both been through war
given this complicated circumstance
I know it's not a one-way street
This love's been like a misplaced street light
making it so the neither of us can sleep,
up thinking about all the possibilities
We never figured it out, but we let it be
Must've been love in the midst of leaves
turning over truths about us, true colors
They showed me you were the one
just before they crumbled
You know I've been looking
for the missing piece to my puzzle
I've tried a lot of different shapes
but they never seem to fit that space
right there in the center of it all
Can't nobody fit that but the original
I know it's a cliché visual,
but there is nothing cliché about us
We've always been authentic so…
it must've been love

What else could it be?
Lust couldn't have saved us
from the avalanche or the sea
I just want to make up
Baby, won't you look at me
Won't you put your hands on me
You're the only man for me
You understand me, you don't judge me
You let me be all the woman I want to be
You never tell me what to wear
You don't question me when my girls take me out
I think we can figure out a way
to make this work now
Must've been love
made it last this long
Must've been love
made me miss you when you're gone
Must've been love
got me holding on strong
Must've been love
made the trees talk in the forest when I was lost
told me to just follow my heart
Must've been love
made me let down my guards
We can go anywhere you want,
nothing is off limits anymore
Must've been love,
when you answered the door...
held me in your arms and said,
"You'll always be my baby girl,
don't you cry no more."

Be Your Star

If you put the sparkle in my life
then don't forget to maintain that
I wish you could borrow my eyes
so you could witness the way that
you make me shine inside
I just want to play back
the moments it felt so right
even though those days passed
I'm ready for new memories
Baby, the moon is beautiful
but it's not you and me
So if you wonder why I'm losing my glow
it's not too hard to see
that stars can't live without a sky to shine in
Where is my piece of eternity to put my light in?
Tell me love, why I'm having trouble flying?
I used to move so natural like…
I was timeless
but the minute I did find him,
everything was different
The hourglass flipped, and I realized…
this is the only chance we get as humans
Reality hit with nobody to pinch me
back to dreamland again
But even the sweetest dream
can't connect me the way he does
when I'm pressed against all his black velvet
and my star heart begins to drip
iridescent reflections of passionate expressions
I've kept within until I found him
Doesn't he get it?
Without him I'm like a nightlight

with no light switch or place to plug it in
Wishing he would harmonize with our design
and like a trillion glow sticks
we could start glowing
all over again…

I told him I'm tired of being a star
with no sky to shine in (shine in)
If he loves me with all my scars
Will he love me when I'm a diamond (shining)
Said baby these days are hard
but I'm trying (crying)
I just want to be your star
even if you're the only one
who sees my light within
Whenever the nighttime comes
like the sky he sends me flying
So I'll be shooting up above
right beside him (wishing)
That I can be his star forever
Shining my brightest (with him)

If you've ever seen a shooting star
from the corners of your eye
But it was too fast for your thoughts
to catch in light-years of time
If you've ever watched the years go by
wondering when you'd catch one again
then you know why people fear
this thing called love when
there are no guarantees
But baby, you found the star in me

So tell me a story about a girl and a boy
who believed they could follow dreams
and show me the way to the honeybees
of our galaxy so they can lead us
to something sweet
if they promise not to sting
Baby, baby you act like you're allergic
to my reaction of your touch
yet the Milky Way's still churning
and mashing this thing up
into a mixture of this special stuff
that makes emotions appear fluorescent
with no way to hide this love
If you'd like, we can turn off all the nights
and just become one
I like us better in the night
when I can shine on the sky of us
and remember what it was
to have your arms carrying me to your heart
when I'm done putting on the light show
and just want to be
the woman you love unconditional
no matter what
You said I will always be beautiful
so I want to be your star with my old soul
I want to be the reason
your sky can't shine if I were to ever go
but... I want to tell you that I won't
if you won't take it to your head
because I don't want to settle for less
than shining for the heavens, *that's what I told him.*

A Muse Called Love

Oh, do the angels flutter
their wings of delicacy
on our tender candy kisses
forever reminding us to be
a special treasure to be cherished within
to shed tears cleansing temples of sin…
become again, angelic
Of every candle melted,
I remember the one that carried
my wish in its womb for my darling
I remember the way that flame grew
and the contractions started
I remember wishing the phone would have rang,
wondering if you were heartless
You know I get lonely at night
Losing myself like a kite with no wind to fly,
tangled in a tree somewhere afar
Our ancient roots told me,
to follow the brightest star
Oh, how I pray you would hold me
in your strong arms
Make me weak
To find, you must seek
To obtain favor, you must be
the one to bless me with the Holy seed
symbolized through
the loveliest ring made just for me
Tell me you adore me
as the rain tumbles from
chambers of a love always wet
You should have forewarned me
of the pain that would ache

with my only cure being your sweat
dripping down your forehead and chest
Crossing deserts just to rescue me
as I shiver,
emotions pouring like tea-pitchers
My knees quiver
at the thought of you coming home
My scars begin to blister,
I'm just a fallen rose
having dreams of honey-filled bubbles
in bathtubs of you and me
Thinking he might as well propose,
since he dug his truth into me,
buried it here beneath time capsules and things
I know he cares, but sometimes a lady has needs
The extra mile darling, is calling your name
If you can hear me, it's not a bargain
There's no sale on this love chain
letter, traveling on a rosebud train
nearly running off the tracks
every time I come back from
imagining you were rubbing my back
with almond oils on your masculine hands
I don't want to be spoiled,
just assigned to God's plans
for the right man to be my right hand
through thick or thin
To remember me when,
the home boys convincing
that your woman doesn't come first
When Satan is mixing drinks,
to delusion you into a curse

and the clock nearly strikes
but just in time you have a rebirth
Just milliseconds away from a lifetime of hurt
but on Grandfather clocks, our hands go around
The stories our ancestors told us of love
still speak in our tongues
The language is unchanging
Darling, you can turn the pages
but each one will reveal another secret
whispered through lip prints that seal
the hidden passage to something so real
that I know you'd be back again
even if you fell off the wheel
You were molded just for me
You have opened the lotus flower in me...
waiting patiently, to be pollinated by my king
Fragile as I'll ever be,
so please be gentle with your touch
"Come Soft To Me," baby...
I'm only a vessel of sweet love
I'm only a butterfly floating
in a puddle of liquid dust
from the wings of lovers
that came before us
I'm only a sunflower
in a garden of violets
standing out modestly
with nowhere to hide this
For the height of our love is much too tall
to be denied for a worldly cause
Increasing spiritually,
is a lesson to be taught

and like a piano instructor,
I'm showing you the keys
If you watch, soon you will be
reading notes on the spot,
ready to compose
our beautiful orchestra
created by a muse called love.

Inkwells of Love

One day we'll look back
to this crazy year, crazy times
Living in this ghetto crib
in this hood, on this block
Have a picnic, sit and swap
"Remember when…" stories
Share war scars in our hearts
You'll ask me if I'm all right…
wipe the tear I'll try to hide
from the corner of my eye
but you'll already know why,
I had to let one go…
The struggle babe, been a trip and we
been through much more than losing a "seed"
Reflecting on adversities the people never see
Some people never wanted us to be
Be happy to see us disagree
Dissing you, you dissing me
Yeah, we took it there…
you know what I mean
Times we'd swear, we're going to up and leave
Emotion flying off the handle
and the damage done
Felt the pain deep in slow motion,
I thought we were really done
But fast forward
here we are
We are…
holding hands
in our car
Jaheim music playing,
sharing thoughts

Confiding in each other,
finally learned to talk
about anything and, everything
Doing more than communicating
We're vibin', love
and I'm in love
more than yesterday
or all the days before
All the make-up love we've made
made me want to start an argument today
Just playing babes
I'm saying babes,
life would have never been the same
if you'd walked out
or I'd packed that suitcase
I can't lie,
did it in my mind
one thousand times
when I…
had too much pride
to let you know
I'd never go
I'll never go
The earth and the heavens know
even my soul
will be searching for you
in the Lord's castle
Until then,
let's experience the joys
of winning every battle, test, and trial
through God's grace
Recognize time is never wasted

through all these mazes
we've had to master
just for this key
I turn in you,
you turn in me
unlocking the next chapter
of a love
written from the inkwells
of eternity.

Pleasing My King

When I think about, *think about*
pleasing my king, *I want to please him*
It sends me on an upward spiral
like a winding staircase to a lighthouse
flipped upside down
Suddenly I'm already at the top
awaiting for your ship to make its stop
I'm here baby, in the brightest light
If I ever left you hypnotized
please know that it's much more divine
Baby, if you look into my eyes
there's much more than hypnosis tricks
I'm genuine
I promise you this for life
There will always be a you and I
This is an us thing, a become one thing
Now let me tell you something...
when I think about, *I think about*
pleasing my king, *I want to please him*
It makes me slip and slide
on a waterfall that rises heaven high
I want to jump with you into the sky
Come up together, breathe the might
of two lovers that reunite each and every time
Now you know I'm a lover,
but I can be your fighter
If any other brother steps to me...
I will disconnect his wires
Leave him dismissed with the rest of the mix
It's nothing personal, just the way it is
I have found my soulmate, yes we do exist
I want to go on a date somewhere elegant

Blow your mind away, put on a sexy dress
I don't want to mess with your head
I just want to be eloquent
in the way I'm expressing
the fluency of our connection
and baby if you're stressing...
I've got a number of ways to show affection
Just want to please my man
I hope you understand
the reason I want you to take my hand
through all of love's seasons
Baby, I swear I can
please my king
Let me please you
You're not dreaming
Let me pinch you
Feel my heart beating?
Baby it's you
Every time I think about
I think about
pleasing my king
I want to please him
It sends me swinging
from one million trees in a forest
where I get lost just to find
that in between these branches
is the story of a man and his wife
A king and queen
He's awaiting the right moment
to pleasure me in any way he can
When he thinks about pleasing me...
the depths of our path have no limits

Horizons dilate and shift
It's like tectonic plates crashing
into the sweetest alliance
But more than that, we are diamonds
cut from the same rock
A natural occurrence,
not artificially simulated
A volcanic eruption bursting with magma
was what pressured this love to exist
We cooled each other down with just one kiss
Now we're ready to be shined and polished
but we will always have a rough edge
and that's okay love, we're only humans
You don't have to be perfect
for me to know your value is worth it
so if you're hurting I'll ease the pain
Babe, I'm still learning love's way
but every day all I know is…
I want to please my king
On my knees I pray this is
what destiny brings
When I think about the possibility
of letting this thing sink,
it becomes real to me
that we must put up the sails
Keep our faith well-groomed
and through all darkness, our love will prevail
During the phases of each rise and fall of sun and moon,
I'll always love and want to please the king in you!

Love Is like This

There may be times when you're apart
Lonely moments can make love hard
My baby's working two jobs, and that's not it...
he's got two classes, two internships
but let me tell you all, *love is like this*
When I get home from the nine-to-five
it's not long before he's crossed my mind
I call him on the phone, he's too busy and I know
I've got to hold it down until he's home,
yes, love is like this
You need to know that love is like this
Every morning, I'm up at six
getting the kids ready so I can make my shift
My man helps me get them to the car, gives me a kiss
then we rushing off to handle business...
oh, love is like this
Did you know that love is like this?
There are times when it feels like
being Mom is just a second job,
getting fed up all by myself
Just praying to God...
give me strength to carry this weight
I'm holding on but so many times...
I've felt my fingers slip
I feel so unequipped
I never knew that love was like this
Any couple whose ever made it has a story to tell
It may not be like ours,
but you can bet they've been through hell
just to keep that piece of heaven through every storm
and this too shall pass soon as he walks through the door.

Mix of Life

She looked at him
and said
"Love, I just don't want
my dreams to pass me by
in this crazy mix of life
and I
know there is so much to do
but all you have to say
is I believe in you
before I go
out there
and make these moves
Tell me I can do the impossible
Build your lady up
before I hit the road
Give me a hug and kiss
just to let me know
'cause love
always wins
even if we don't."

Ask any successful person
how many failed attempts
it took to reach a level
of accomplishments
Let me tell you about,
losing yourself to find yourself
Writer's block, when the words
don't flow from your inkwell
Watching life visions
trickle down the wishing well

Going back to drawing boards
and dreaming bigger than before
Praying on a plan of action well beyond yours
Going from completely discouraged
to finally finding courage to soar
then falling flat on your face
a few times more
It's all a test of resilience
that you must endure

Trust me when I tell you
your dreams can pass you by
Talents can be wasted
but there's no more wasting mine
Been doing this too long
just to give it up
My life calling, keeps on calling
so now I'm picking up
They can diss me and dismiss me
but God picked me
among the chosen ones
Despite all of my downfalls
I recognize now, life is
one lifetime too short
cliché as that sounds,
I can't live in bondage anymore
My metamorphosis begins now
without remorse
so if you want to believe the rumors
but defamation of character
was not my greatest war

I've been through worse,
did you forget I'm a survivor?
I understand…
because there were times
when I forgot myself
but standing in the way of God's plans
is standing in the way of yourself
Now excuse me, if you couldn't tell
I'm on my way to sharing a testimony
that will help someone else

There isn't nothing like a praying man
and there sure isn't nothing
like a praying woman
but the power is in the spirit,
not the flesh of our hands
And there will be times,
you have to do it for yourself
There are moments in life
we are challenged to look within
when there is no one else
serving as an intercessor on your behalf
Good as it feels for someone to have your back
God is the driving force
behind the scenes on your path
He's the one who will bless you with
the king or queen to tell you that
they believe in you
before you go out there
and make these moves.

Glimmer of Hope

Tender Love
Splendor touch
Entrance to suns
Shine like the moon
Bright night smile
No time for denial
Embracing
Escalating
Growth is our concentration
Majoring in love,
taking classes like "Patience"
Working day shifts
Sometimes late shifts
Schedules split
But our souls shift one inch
closer together every day
Merging in a lane named "Forever"
without delay
Walking through traffic
with invisible protection
I stopped being passive
to his affection
after trying to sever
our connection with my only
good reasons being my own
Gave God the wheel
said "Here, take control!"
And now we're here
driving on this road
We can feel the pull
and when I feel his tug,
it's reassurance of what I know...

we are falling in love
beyond physical attraction
and I never gave it up
but friendship has fastened
the clasp of us
like a locket implanted
deep in our chests
Funny how being honest
can lead us to happiness
Feelings expressed
always with the realness
Every day we connect
even if it's for, twenty-six minutes
when we're handling business, that's all right
Whatever God has in mind, I will sign
The only print that's fine
is the print of his love in my eyes
reading between
Some people still can't see
but we've been put on a label,
called "Heavenly"
As he takes the lead,
this is clearly the makings
of eternity.

Love Pieces

Pieces of me and you
morphing into new
shapes of us
Recreating love
An innovative love
Changing when we must
as these obstacle courses
continue to show up, we must
strategically plan every move and motion
stripping our beliefs of self-absorption
In each and every dream,
I do support him
Even when we disagree
there is growth
through every point explored in
those spaces of time
searching for the right fit
With so many details in the mix...
sometimes the big picture can be hard to see
but we've made this commitment
to be honored infinitely
no matter how hard it may be
When in matrimony,
there are no one-way streets
so we clear our minds
of these one-way thoughts
selfishly clogging entryways
where our souls will seek new beginnings
branching off of roots that run deep
Only his love can nourish my needs
In a world so congested by weeds,
we need the strength to breakthrough

as this warfare is constant
with methods of spiritual strangulation
Anyone in love must come prepared
for a manipulator better known as Satan
with an ultimate goal
to breakup happy homes
claiming sinful souls
Divorce papers
make the Devil smile,
believe that
But most of all…
believe in the Lord's protection
over vows kept
no matter how challenging
the levels of this puzzle can get
We must not
We cannot
We will not forget
how to stand on love
even in the mess
Let's stand up, love
loose the fear in our chests
as we find inner peace
and come to be
one more piece
closer to
a moment
complete.

Dissolve Me

I'm dissolving into oneness
as your tears form a pond
around my feet,
cleansing me of impurities
as I become perfection
through your eyes reflecting
a mental paradise
where roses have thorns
that feel like pleasure
as they prick our minds
Your mind, my mind
dissolving into a secret life
where our spirits fly like kites
and the wind is our dear friend
witnessing us unite in marriage,
dressed in white clouds
and raindrop crowns
as every element in creation
announces us husband and wife now
Destiny written vows
Sun of your moon, moon of your sun
I loved you since the first day,
I tasted wet stars on your tongue
as you dipped them into the golden dust
that leads to a sacred sea
exceeding all expectation
of how heaven must be
Lungs began breathing at the same speed
Oxygen became our favorite candy
and we developed a sweet tooth
for the gift of each tree
that bears good fruits to nurture our seed

planted in the womb of divinity
as you dissolve into my knees
I feel weak, I can't speak... just be
Jump into me like piles of autumn leaves
Love intuitively in warm colors of intimacy
Fall free into the middle of me
as the center of you make us complete
fully dissolved until it's just "we"
melting into one eternity
To rip us apart would be blasphemy at best
Never shall we curse that which we were blessed
Never second guess God's intent
or forget this spiritual quest
where we found the key to true oneness
was dissolving in our flesh.

This Love

This ain't no chalkboard love
so hold your erasers for that
new school wash-off stuff
That slip like sand through your fingers
soon as the tide comes in, junk
No offense, but real love's essence
compare not to the worldly connection
of hormones interlocked
just until the locksmith
known as time shows up
Some folk, will never know love
Never grow up
to relinquish wandering eyes
for a value so divine
as a man finding his wife
Letting rappers sell them
illusions of happiness
Pimping the devil's lie
into vulnerable minds
not fastened with spiritual intelligence
welcoming ignorance instead
where wisdom was intended
Our new age generations
only think they are content with
the conditioning they've been,
brainwashed to believe
but deep down in the soul
of every human being
is a voice that screams,
"Love me!"
beyond the objectified,
over-sexualized imagery

constantly swarming us,
promising sweet honey
with no warning of the deadly stings
that lustfulness will bring
I peep the facts…
diseases, broken homes,
this baby daddy, momma crap
Number one reason for divorces
be adultery, so we ask…
where has real love gone?
But it's right here…
living in spirits of those who've
survived the hypnosis
Unaffected, protected
by the creator of love everlasting
Access granted to the few and far between
So now, you see
why him and I are no
"Will they make it?" mystery
Our destiny already been solved and authorized
Even heaven holds a place for us
so please don't sound surprised
when this love surpasses
the limits and boundaries
set by mankind
when even "Until death do us part,"
doesn't apply
'cause this love was designed
with eternal instincts
that kick in even in
the absence of physical vessels
This love does not need skin

in order to transcend earthly levels
so please do edify
the reading of vows for us
because love like this doesn't part
but rather begins
in a new form
only known to God.

The Fountain in Us

I told him, to come hold me
because it's cold outside
So he wrote me a secret love letter
It said, "Close your eyes and remember…"
My taste buds answer "I do!"
How could I forget, the flavor of you?
The kiss that sealed my lips with
the most divine affection I've ever known
I miss it like a good habit
It's not always an addiction, sometimes it's gold
Sometimes it's soul
Sometimes it's beautiful
Sometimes it's okay to lose control
and be vulnerable to a new sequence
to have you feeling like you never did
Everything is different with this new "television"
The antennas of two lovers, radiating vibrant colors
but at the bottom of our hearts will always be
the old-fashioned parts of you and me
the black and white version of our memories
You're black, and I'm white and I still believe
that one day your hand in mine won't make people angry
They want things to be the way they used to be
They wanted things to change in but a few ways
We could drink from the same fountains
and pick out our own bus seats
but if we ever should have babies or get married,
we would see that hate can be a black or white seed
planted on either side where they divide the line
I wonder if Rosa Parks would agree
with the way we undermine the courage she did find
to stand up and be different despite all the odds

Despite the talk, despite imprisonment
Well, just make sure it's a heart-shaped lock
with a keyhole to which he can behold
the skeleton key created by God
Just make sure that when you quote the scripture
as your reason to vouch for racist thoughts
that you remember unevenly yoked
was not about our skin colors,
it was about being yoked with Jesus
Just remember that when we make love
not to call us sinners based on skin pigments
Just remember that every time you judge,
that by the judge you are being measured
so I hope you measure up to your own poison
I hope that you don't overdose on it
I hope that you don't miss the boat
to cross over to your anointing
I hope that you can see us as more than skin
More than a white woman "stealing" black men
More than a couple with biracial kids
More than two people rebelling against the system
But how can we rebel against something
we never did believe in to begin with?
If you want to talk about revolution,
then you're looking at it
Please have no confusion about our happiness
Don't label it "jungle fever",
or a white chick chasing the black fix
Just know that behind our physical vessels,
we are nothing but humans
We come from the same place you did,
a womb inside of a woman

While we may have ancestry
from different continents
in terms of biological science
Remember that it was all predicted
before we ever existed
as breathing infants in a land of laws
that leave us convicted,
guilty, and charged
for crimes we never did commit
based on the laws of God
It's in the book, I just delivered it
so get the message and remember
that I will always remember him
Forget your perversion
as we were referring
to the nights he held me
and our world started turning
Merging, converting,
to spin on one axis
and in the end, our love
was all that really mattered
as we drink from the same fountain
no matter how the system new age "lynches" us.

My Poetry, Him, and Me

If my poetry is the key to his heart
then that's beautiful
Some say art isn't who we really are
and that's truthful for some folks
who only brushstroke and bust flows
just to blow smoke
But for me, each word I ever wrote
beholds the bottom most parts of my soul
and so, if he finds his way to elope
through one million love poems
then I know...
he's the one, to leave me unplugged
like a Lauryn Hill show
On that note...
I'll keep reading him poems
I'll keep our love lit with this glow
I'll communicate things that always flow
a little sweeter in the context of
similes and metaphors
mixed up with "keep it simple"
and I'll open the doors to his temple
one syllable at a time
until it's inevitable
and cannot be denied
he was made from God's mold
to be mine
and he doesn't just
love the way I write
but he loves me
because I am my poetry.
And he loves me especially...

when I openly serenade him
with poetic butterfly wings
that seduce his peaks on
levels mentally, sexually,
emotionally, and spiritually
Now, that's peace and… love
in a way beyond folks who speak
"Peace and Love" just to fit the poetic glove
but he fits me like pens and pads,
like ink and diaries,
notebooks and Microsoft,
writing books and worshiping God,
raindrops and candle lights,
like an eraser top
when I want to change that line,
like poems written since I was a child
He fits me like forgiveness during life's trials,
like lipstick tracing my smile,
like perfect kisses, we're always in style
He goes with everything in my wardrobe,
inside and out
He fits the castle of my mind, body, soul
like a new house designed just for me
He fits me like home sweet home after a show
when I just need my king
to bathe me and massage my feet
Take me to a place where no one can hurt me
and love me like he loves my poetry
because I am her and she is me
and I am ready so I hope he's ready
to set free our destiny so it can be…

so it can breathe beyond poetry
Baby these words are not just words,
they are keys
to every door of you and me
and the reason you love my poetry
is because you are the man between
each love sheet, every love piece
Before we even met, you loved me
Soon you will see my poems
are flesh of your flesh, bone of your bone
But for now, lie your head on my chest
and listen to this new one I wrote
I hope you like it…
pressed like a rose in your soul
I promise each poem was chose by hands
that control a love eternal
For this is only the beginning of our journey
as we bind together as one,
forming the autobiography of our love
with many sequels, chapters, and pages
we keep for ourselves
There will come a day,
when nothing matters in our physical shells
and all we see is the love we've felt
when you first fell in love
with our inkwell.

Unconditionally He

He loves me
When I say, "I need to lose weight!"
He says, "Baby you look fine!"
When I say,"My skin is breaking out,"
he says, "You're human, it's alright."
When I say,"I'm PMS'ing,"
he says, "Baby I understand, at least I try…
let me go to the store,
get your lady things, the brand you like,
chocolate coconut milk ice cream,
Midol, and those heating pads
to ease the cramps and clear your mind."
When I am feeling bitchy,
he brings out my softer sides
He knows exactly what I like
He even takes me shopping sometimes
Not to buy my love, but to ease my mind
He knows fashion kicks it with my, artistic side
and he likes to kick it with me anytime…
sweatpants and a tee, or dressed up looking right
He knows I have flaws, but he sees beyond
He knows I have heart, and he knows where I'm from
He knows this life has brought me pain
He wants to clear my thoughts of thinking these ways
He doesn't want insecurities
although he loves mine, beautifully
If I gain a little weight
If I don't look perfect every day
If another girl walks by trying to mesmerize
Thoughts of him and I making love pop up
as he looks into my eyes
and remembers the colors of our love

Baby boy, you spoil me...
I don't want to let you go
When I have cried about things,
tears other people will never see,
you let me vent the ache until my heart can beat
You don't deny me of the right to be
a woman with feelings and needs
When I confide in you about the things
men have done to me
When I tell you I'm a survivor,
you thank the Lord that you found me
and I thank Him more that you did seek...
that He gave you some kind of sign to read,
that you flowed with the tide
even when it was scary,
that you want to be a part of my family
and have become a branch on the tree
we together climb to the highest one
Yes, we're sitting in the tree of love...
kissing underneath the moon and sun,
hiding from everyone just to be alone
You give me your jacket when I get cold
You open my door when we're on the go
You wash my hair in the bathtub
You feed me sweet fruits between bed sheets
That's how I know that...
unconditionally he loves me
No matter what anyone thinks
No matter how many times
groupies try to make our ship sink
No matter the rumors, the lies, the schemes
You're all I need

Just me, you, and our dreams
and most of all the Lord always
So speak now or forever hold your peace
but this love is a two way street
We bounce back and forth
like a basketball team
Ever since the day he laid eyes on me,
he wanted to wife me
He likes me
He loves me
He thinks I'm so pretty
He sees the soul within my soul,
the keys in between the keys
I'm his piano, his fingers play me perfectly
This love is a tranquil spring
found in between the rock of him and me
We open our mouths and drink until we're filled…
overflowed with purity, beauty is all he sees
underneath my clothes or in these jeans
Finally, I can breathe!
Been holding out for a true love
between two love
becoming one reflection of God
with no limit or conditions
to make this love stop.

I Left Him Speechless

I left him speechless at the drop of a dime
I picked up the pieces she forgot were behind
His words were unspoken though I read his lips
I heard them like potion the moment we kissed
Pressed firm as a prayer; forming the key
He caressed my hair, through our unborn destiny
Together, we unlocked the gates of paradise
We would not break by the parasites
Destruction amongst us, burdens we carried
turned to nothing but dust urgent we bury
Let it dissolve in the soil, manifesting next spring
What evolves will be royal with blessings it brings
Deception was her name, unpleasant was her game
You were her peasant, her song you sang
But our music plays with the wind,
acoustics made upon the heavens
Our hearts we sold to heartless souls,
on beat-less chests we rested heads
until the night we intertwined
We were rose vines
tangled within each other's stems
Angelic lovers God can't condemn
Our marriage binding at first glimpse
Karats couldn't define this circumstance
For I left him speechless at the drop of a dime
Yes, love is a weakness only strong will survive.

Too Tired

When I'm much too tired to walk,
will you carry me home?
When I am too weak to keep up my guards,
will you guard my heart on your own?
When I can't stand anymore,
will you catch me in your arms?
When all the harvesting has me worn out,
will you console?
When you see my skin hardening
will you rub lotion, keep it soft?
When my body needs a scrubbing,
will you run the bathwater?
Sponge me down in a tub of rose petals,
light a candle and tell my eyes to close
When the world has hurt me so,
will you hold me close?
Will you see me as just a body,
underneath my clothes?
Will you understand that behind this skin,
is a woman's soul?
She cries and says,
"Baby, I don't want to live this life alone."
Will you secure my thoughts,
Tell me, "Darling, you won't."

Flower of Eternal Love

Only a real man can emotionally connect
to the revelations of a real woman
when she expresses things so complex
like how she sacrifices
four children later, a stillborn first
with three survivors
Her body wears the marks,
permanent war paint
Although she is his warrior,
only human roots thrive within her
The fragility of her nature is necessary
The moments where he can nurture, are destined to be
Kiss away one million tears you didn't cause,
only then can you call yourself a man
His fingertips communicate love to her skin
healing power more potent than plants
She understands the meaning
of the movement of his hands
like brushstrokes on a canvas
only the original artist can decipher
He meditates on the spaces
between her heartbeats,
taking in the moment
like when a poet pauses,
using brief silence as a tool for saturation
Nature does the same if you listen...
and he is soaking wet in the rhythm
of her creation
His body penetrates her
Her soul, penetrates him
as their shadows tell the story
of a man who loves his woman

without conditions
For he knows eternal love
is otherwise a lost cause
So he sacrifices,
loosens his grip on
flesh-bound ways
for the way of the spirit
as a new flower buds
on the oneness of them.

Sweet Nothings

He walks with me
like wind walks with leaves…
blows my mind, and then I leave,
floating softly away from the tree
to the ground beneath his feet
where he comes down just to worship me
and then we rise to royalty
He whispers to me, "You are killing me softly!"
I whisper back, "Death must be a treat,"
because every time he dies he brings life into me
and then into him I breathe…
Sing me a song from the treetops of your heart
I want to swing from the highest branch
Touch the sky as I look into your eyes
Drink the syrup from your deepest love
Join roots until we become one
Watch the birds fly by on your bluest day
Be the wind to whisper to you
that everything is okay.

I Used to Dream of You

I used to dream of you...
prayed on my knees that you'd
be here soon
but it was never soon enough
and yet somehow,
it was also never too late

I wallowed in the tears
that always escaped
when nobody was there
to witness my pain
Drenching myself
in the concept of
a love that never came

I wrote one thousand poems
from the passions of my heart
Dug deep down into my soul
and found love underneath
my nails, as though
I'd gardened in its yard

Planted seeds of us in places
only we could find
Leaving only subtle traces
that would lead you
to these dreams of mine

Dreams I'd harvest
and grow, each day
Dreams that kept me whole
when reality seemed to scrape

at the remnants of
gems I held precious -
the gems of love I so treasured

See, there were moments
where my faith wavered
and I wondered
if I'd ever sail again
Felt myself going under,
yes I remember when

You rescued me
from becoming a prisoner
to my own dreams
You gave me a love
that had fully blossomed into reality
Reminding me that this journey
was never purposeless
like some silly thought, I thought
would one day come to be

Nourishing all my needs,
you brought me to the surface
with a kiss so perfect
that I thought this was all
just another one of my dreams
The dreams of love
that would flood my being,
creating a sea for you to cross
just to get to me
But this was finally that thing
I'd searched and waited for half my life

That thing the old folks told me...
I'd just know it, when it's right
and it's just like...
better than anything
I've ever dreamt
Something so serene,
my inner peace
can breathe again

You darling,
are my best friend
Soon to be, husband
and there is nothing I wouldn't do
just to see that gaze in your eyes
A gaze as though you see the sky
of beautiful stars when you look at me

Stars that show you
the way into my heart
where those dreams used to beat
but now it's truly you and me
and we're much more
than just the seeds of us
that once grew inside my dreams.

Love Refugees

Wicked sun piercing between
one cracked windowpane
we peeved but never fixed
In an otherwise dark room,
are two bodies lit by flickering beams
A work of art blooms as these
uninvited light tricks permits
traces of your eyes and lips to reappear
Highlighting basic lines
and textures of this skin we fear
Exploiting our most human flaws
Kisses adorning each other's scars
transformed into precious jewels
to be worn with confidence in this room
tucked away within the city of a concrete jungle
where real lovers are an endangered species
but like refugees, we flee
We made love in a bed of broken dreams
as the pieces came together to re-create a reality
sweeter than the aspirations that grew
from roots of inspiration
and merely didn't survive above the surface
where anything so beautiful would be suffocated,
crippled, trampled upon like pearls before swine
and with our broken dreams, came broken hearts
but somehow all of this broken, made ... us.

Love was Born

As her fingertips glide over the blinds...
softly opening them, she doesn't pry...
Letting in the sunshine
feels like a nice thought that warms her mind
She sighs, pleasured by each ray of light
Her beloved sees her, but stays quiet
admiring her essence in its natural form
noticing the way her silhouette changes every morn
growing inside her first born
witnessing the way she begins to nurture
everything around her
Taking extra care of even their home plants
as their different shadows dance on her porcelain skin
She's a queen of affection and spiritual connections

More than a child, she's expecting blessings
Feeling God's presence stronger than before
She knows their love was destined forever more
She leaves her man breathless and secure
He is sure she **is** the one whose roots stem from his rib
She is pure even if there are people who call her tainted
She reminds him of something angelic
but he's lost of words and though he has the urge,
he doesn't bother her but rather, cherishes the God in her
Just before he goes to work he kisses her,
looks into her eyes as though they are made of stained glass
and tells her he loves her in a way that reminds her
of wind chimes on a spring day, fresh breeze at last...

She knows she has the key to the secrets of real love
He knows that she is the deepest woman made of ancient seas
His sails are up, ready to travel her heart...

in the most vicious storm or brightest sun
He trusts in the Son
Doesn't concern himself with people who judge their love
but rather yearns for help from God
because God is love

For how many times has mankind's advice hurt people
who receive and follow without God as their guide?
He thinks that anyone who cannot see the beauty
between he and she is surely blind
She was crafted for his sight
and everything she is inside is part of him like
the rain is part of the sky
and the ground is part of the earth
like the baby within her
awaiting its birth into the world
Boy or girl?

He ponders from time-to-time
She tells him it's a daughter, brings tears to his eyes
as he imagines a little girl who resembles her
basking in the beauty living in the vessel of her
A beauty created by, him, her, and God
fills him with joyousness
He's made her a Mom...
He thinks she becomes more gorgeous each minute
that her heart throbs with new life
within his willed to be new wife
Silently he gives thanks for this precious time
Sometimes he prays over her in the morning time,
glorifying God for a gift so divine
He wants to give her everything

but does realize that most of all...
his loyalty and heart while leading her
on a Godly walk are what matters
when there is nothing else
He vows to treasure her
through sickness and health
Love her the way Christ loved the church
as the Word orders and tells
If he could tell you how it felt
when God spoke into his chest,
it was like a miracle had become
of his emptiness
where others left him vacant
real love was sanctioned

Always a friend but...
now a man to change her
last name to his
A man she can pray with,
grow wise and gray with
Conquer life's pain with
Get through labor on that due date with
Feel safe with and worry no more
For he is the window that opened
when God closed a door
She is the soul chosen for him long before
they even knew love was born.

My Heart

If my heart had wings, it would always be with you
Visiting you, tending to you, praying over you
Protecting you, guiding you away from the evils in this world
Blocking every wrong path, guarding every temptation
Loving you in your most pitiful moments
Whispering beautiful things in your ears
to channel out the ugly things coming from their mouths
My heart would give up a wing
just so yours could reciprocate in the same fashion
Unconditionally, rain or shine
In "glam" mode or completely natural
I only hope your heart would see me the way I see you
Love me the way I love you
If your heart had wings…
tell me love, where would it fly to?
Would it even matter whose heart was whose,
if we are so divinely connected?
Would your heart find its sanctuary place
inside my chest, beating life into my flesh?
As my body accepts, determines it not to be a foreign object
I'd awaken, feeling about myself the way you feel about me
in love with every living cell and every inch of my body
Looking with my own eyes, yet somehow seeing through yours
Only then would I understand,
what those three words you speak mean
Smiling, knowing… I'm the girl of your dreams for real
Even in my most pitiful moment
Even if my heart had no wings
Even when the only thing I knew how to be, was human
Even then, even now, even more.

#NoFilterLove

You make me feel like
the prettiest face in the crowd
Don't get me wrong, plenty fly ladies
with "Mani's" and "Pedi's" locked down
but when you and me are in town,
street lights shine brighter
Old couples still in love smile with delight at us
Fountain pennies get extra lucky,
granting wishes just because
Stars show out early just to rehearse,
twinkling in the rhythm of the music made
every time you look at me that way...
attentively with an intensity
that suspended me in mid-sentence, see?
I forgot what we, where we, left off
Lost my thought, found myself on a higher plane
floating wondering how we landed here,
feet mingling underneath a table for two
The only candle still lit when the others blew
Our love has that effect
Apple crisp tastes sweeter
like love was in the air when they baked it
The music play-list is tailored to fit,
all our jams play back-to-back
Nights like this were meant to last
However many people been walking past,
your eyes tend to fixate only on me
Could it be the little black dress
or high heels on my feet
or simply, the way you feel around me?
Like the most handsome man I've ever seen
in a room flooded by the finest suits you could dream...

I'm sitting here with the man of my dreams
The waitress asks how did we first meet
We both answer, "Poetry!"
Didn't know it then, we'd be married with a family
but I know more than ever now,
we made the right choice
'cause fate just puts a move on us...
pulls out all the stops and whistles for us
Fairy tales might get jealous over us
leaving trails of real love wherever we go,
signing "was here" on waves of energy
Destiny longs to be in our presence
We may not be celebrities,
but we have something God-sent
Ask me if I cared what people said
Take lessons on my confidence
More woman than I've ever been
Never stopped being passionate
but when others left me for dead,
he stood by my side, saw past the mess
My friend, my confidant long before my husband
and can't nothing stand in our way
when sunbeams reach further just to touch our skin
through blinds where two morning lovers kiss
and I love his kiss and I love his lips
We woke up like this, on some #NoFilter status
For the record yes, our love's the "baddest"...
don't need no extras, it's just perfect as is.

Good Love

Let's go to our quiet destination
Grab a bite, share some conversation
Phones on silent, attention solely
and completely on this intimate occasion
Tonight, I saw that spark in your eyes
like when we first met
I felt that feeling like when
our spirits were connected
That first night vibe…
that extra sweet taste of pre-butterflies
before you'd made a total honeysuckle of my soul
and I'd run but never quite hide
from your attempts to pollinate my mind
as we'd politic and share insight…
newfound wisdom,
random stuff you think up at two fifteen a.m.
trading spiritual perspectives
Despite all the times we went in separate ways,
each way led to the day we'd say
what we'd been meaning to say
I've been meaning to say…
I still love you as much plus more
I'd rather argue with you any day of the week
although I prefer we pray and make peace
I'd rather fight the good fight with you
than make love every night to the wrong dude
You're right for me no matter how many times we disagree
The minute you say, "Honey, come here next to me,"
I'm there, ready to sort it out, just promise you'll play fair
I'm not into the blame game, I'm into positive change
I don't take it lightly, changing my last name
My intention is to build with you

Continue the chapters of love
our ancestors bookmarked in our hearts
as we pick up where they left off
This love is the train you don't want to get off
Joyriding with you, I enjoy riding with you
I want to lean over and kiss you right now
in front of everyone or no one
What difference would it make?
I want our love engraved in the energy
of every place we set foot in
I don't care who's looking
It's time for love to be seen again
It's time for us to dream again
Be the boy meets girl again
It's time to stand on ashes of broken homes
and then vow this love unbreakable!
Rebels against the statistic
Passion burning for what we believe in
Willing to defend what's ours
While understanding it belongs to God first
A love sanctioned by Him could never be cursed
For what it's worth...
I only hope to share more moments like this
Smiling, admiring, basking in each other's light
Have me like... "I really had a good time tonight,
let's do this again sometime,"
as you grab me closely and plant one on me
on some sexy foot up, back arched, cinema-ready stuff
Darn... I never thought we could be this in love!

ABOUT THE AUTHOR

Born in Connecticut, Tabitha Marie Long, better known on stage as Ms. Tabu, is a well-rounded writer and performance poet, writing her first poem at the young age of ten. She then discovered a new gift for rhythm and lyricism at thirteen and has been songwriting ever since. Not to mention her theatrical roots that stem from early childhood and have grown around her wordplay and envelop her artistic demeanor on stage.

For the audience, witnessing the real life inspired acts of Ms. Tabu can be like watching a clip from a dramatically enchanting play. In some of her writings, she focuses on interracial issues with pieces such as "I'm Not Worth Your Stereotypes," as she passionately promotes diversity through her nicely seasoned delivery of words. Both in and out of her artistry, Ms. Tabu is a humanitarian who advocates for social justice and equal rights. From her viewpoint, it is through her honesty and courageousness that others can be reached.

Extremely versatile, she also writes of many other subjects, such as ones pertaining to love, spirituality, and family. She takes lovers of her craft into her world to share her heart with them. Her work echoes of a soul being delivered from personal struggles, as she heals through each page of her life. She is both hip-hop and soulful with a touch of a woman's manifesto and a Free Verse style that lets her navigate from poetry to prose, making her a phenomenal performer.

Ms. Tabu has been featured at countless events and venues, mainly between Connecticut and New York City. On September 23rd 2010, Ms. Tabu successfully presented the grand debut of her show, "MIC2SOUL," which showcased new artists on a monthly basis.

A woman of many goals, Ms. Tabu is currently in the process of writing new content for *A Voyage to Love*, what will be the third book of the "Love Passages" series. She also has plans to record several Spoken Word albums based on the material in her books.

It would be easy for someone to assume that a person so artistically equipped would lack humility, but Ms. Tabu humbly perceives herself as a vessel with a purpose to deliver messages through her craft. She is on a God-given mission not only to give voice to the voiceless, but to instill healing and growth in people through relating experiences.

THANK YOU

Thank you for reading *Inkwells of Love*, the second book of the "Love Passages" series! Because reviews are critical in spreading the word about books, please leave a brief review expressing what you enjoyed most about it on Amazon, Barnes & Noble, or Goodreads.

***For my eBook lovers, Kindle and Nook editions are also available.

If you missed the first book of the series, *Hot Pink Nail Polish and a Broken Heart*, get it now on Amazon or Barnes & Noble.

Stay tuned for the release of the third book of this ongoing series, *A Voyage to Love*.

Also by *Author* Ms. Tabu:
CROSS POINTS:
The Poetic Diary of Ms. Tabu

CONNECT

Want to know when I release new books and have book signings or special appearances? Here are some ways to stay updated:

Like me on Facebook:
www.facebook.com/MsTabu

Visit my website:
www.MsTabu.com

Follow me on Twitter:
@OfficialMsTabu

Follow me on Instagram:
@MsTabuOfficial